SO-AJY-462

Green
Cleaning

pil

Publications International, Ltd.

WRITER: **Christine Halvorson** is the author of *Solve It With Salt and Vinegar, 100s of Helpful Hints: Practical Uses for Arm & Hammer*® *Baking Soda,* and *The Home Hints Calendar 2000*. She also coauthored *Amazing Uses for Brand-Name Products* and *Clean & Simple: A Back-to-Basics Approach to Cleaning Your Home*. Christine has contributed to many publications, including *The Old Farmer's Almanac,* and national magazines such as *Asthma, Yoga for Everybody,* and *The Lutheran*. She works as a freelance writer from her home in Hancock, New Hampshire.

CONTRIBUTING WRITER: **Erika Swanson Geiss**, M.A., is an art historian and freelance editor. She has worked at the Museum of Fine Arts, Boston, where she was a contributing author on *Monet, Renoir and the Impressionist Landscape*. She has also written *The Right Words for Any Occasion* and *The Passion of Christ* for Publications International, Ltd. Currently she is a curatorial consultant at the Charles H. Wright Museum of African American History in Michigan.

COVER ILLUSTRATION: **Shutterstock**

CONTRIBUTING ILLUSTRATOR: **Meredith Hamilton**

FACTUAL VERIFICATION: **Marci McGrath** and **Chris Smith**

Louis Weber, CEO
Publications International, Ltd.
7373 North Cicero Avenue
Lincolnwood, Illinois 60712

Permission is never granted for commercial purposes.

ISBN-13: 978-1-4127-1682-6
ISBN-10: 1-4127-1682-9

Manufactured in U.S.A.

8 7 6 5 4 3 2 1

Library of Congress Control Number: 2008933281

"Housekeeping ain't no joke."

—Louisa May Alcott, *Little Women*

CONTENTS

GOING GREEN

Recently while on a camping vacation, I used the campground's public shower facilities. I clumsily dropped my black pants onto the shower's tile floor; the pants instantly turned a ghastly Halloween orange. I realized, to my dismay, that the floor had just been mopped with some kind of bleach-based

product. While I was quite happy that as a public facility it was being thoroughly cleaned, I was also worried—if the cleaner had the power to leach color from cloth, what could it be doing to my bare feet?

Similarly, most people want their home to be a clean and pleasant place to live. We don't want germs— especially other people's germs—invading our space. Still, we don't want to achieve those goals by donning a hazmat suit and filling our power hoses with chemicals strong enough to remove the enamel from our teeth.

The toxins found in everyday cleaning products not only have an effect on our health—children, especially, are vulnerable—but also the well-being of our planet. We live in a time when approximately 70 percent of household waste is recyclable, but only about 32 percent is actually reused. We as responsible consumers need to know what's in the products we use, and how they affect those around us. And, as toxic cleaners drain into water supplies and plastic bags continue to pack our landfills, we need to realize that the choices we make do have a lasting impact on the planet.

It is possible to achieve a sanitary and pleasant cleanliness in the home without owning an arsenal of chemically laced cleaning products. I've been doing this kind of "green" cleaning in my own home for a decade now, using products and methods designed to be easier on the environment. Over time and through experimentation, I realized that a few basic, safe products could pretty much clean anything I needed cleaned. Not only are these products better for the environment and my family's health, they are inexpensive, and, well, just *simpler.* My cupboards no longer runneth over with different cleaning products for every task imaginable. Better yet, I didn't need to go out and replace the original toxic cleaners with another arsenal of so-called "earth-friendly" cleaning products and packages.

Breaking It Down

Many people are familiar with the environmental mantra: "Reduce, reuse, and recycle." Note that the first rule is *reduce.* This means that less stuff should be consumed all around, even items labeled "environmentally friendly" or "green." While green products are certainly becoming easier to find—many can be found in your favorite grocery or discount store—logic still holds that just because you *can* buy them doesn't necessarily mean that you *should* buy them.

For the most part, I clean my home with nothing but baking soda, vinegar, and salt, with the occasional lemon added for scent. Every now and again, I expand to include borax, ammonia, or dish soap. Now, I don't say this to be self-righteous—for me, changing to a "less is more" attitude has saved time, money, shelf space, and sanity.

Making the Switch

Thinking about using green cleaning techniques in your home? Start by asking yourself some questions:

- How many cleaning products does the world really need?
- What does one product do that the others can't?
- How much energy goes into making those so-called "earth-friendly" products?
- Where are these products manufactured, by whom, and how far do they travel to get to you?
- How are those products packaged, as compared to what you currently use?

In this book, we will provide you with some general guidelines on getting rid of the harshest cleaning products in your home and offer green ways you can accomplish your everyday cleaning tasks. Along with baking soda, salt, vinegar, and lemon, a few other surprising, nontoxic ingredients will be making cameo appearances. We will also demonstrate how best to declutter your home and how to recycle and reuse some of the throwaways. After a good once-over, you'll find that having a green home is better for the planet as well as your peace of mind.

GETTING STARTED

You may have a certain idea of what "going green" might mean for yourself and your home. In this book, we'll define green cleaning as using products and processes that won't harm your family's health and may be better for the environment than many common commercial cleaners.

If your house is like the average American household, you probably have approximately three to ten gallons of hazardous products stocked in your home to use for cleaning purposes. By hazardous we mean products that can cause physical—and environmental—harm if used incorrectly.

The following items are some of the household cleaning culprits deemed hazardous. Let's call them the **Terrible Ten:**

- Drain cleaners
- Oven cleaners
- Toilet cleaners
- Spot removers
- Silver and other metal polishes
- Furniture polishes
- Cleansers and powdered cleaners
- Window cleaners
- Bleach
- Liquid cleaners

Take a good look under your sink and in your laundry room. Read the labels of any cleaning products you find. If you own any of the products mentioned above in the Terrible Ten, you're likely to discover ammonia and bleach listed in the ingredients. Since ammonia and bleach are so commonplace in our everyday cleaning products, let's give them a closer look.

Bleach really is a somewhat miraculous substance. It makes whites whiter, and it can get mold and mildew out of the bathroom shower in a flash. Sure, bleach has its useful

properties; for instance, it is incredibly helpful when cleaning flood-damaged homes, keeping unhealthy and destructive mold at bay.

But remember those black pants of mine that turned orange? Bleach literally erased the dye from those pants—that's how powerful it is. When mixed with other cleaners and chemicals (ammonia, for one), bleach can become lethal. Sure, your mother and grandmother may have used it around the home in all kinds of ways, but today we are more aware of what bleach may be doing to our water supply, the atmosphere, and our bodies. There are pros to using bleach, but there are also health risks involved; take the initiative to do some research and decide for yourself. For now, however, why take chances?

Eco-facts

According to the Publishers Weekly Web site, the United States alone burns 10,000 gallons of gasoline per second.

Ammonia is another ingredient that shows up in many of those household cleaning products on the Terrible Ten list. Usually citrus or other additives disguise its rather sharp scent and vapors. Have you ever been cleaning with ammonia and suddenly gotten a little light-headed? There's a reason for that—ammonia turns into a gas that is very irritating to the

AMMONIA AND CHLORINE BLEACH: A DEADLY COCKTAIL

There are many bleaching agents used in cleansers, including hydrogen peroxide, but chlorine bleach is the most common. The combination of chlorine bleach and ammonia is deadly and is often erroneously called "mustard gas." While the combination does produce toxic chloramines, it is not technically the mustard gas of chemical warfare, such as was used in both the First and Second World Wars. Various reactions can occur from the accidental mixing of the two ingredients, depending upon the concentration and ratios of each. All reactions are dangerous, however, so avoid mixing them.

Always make sure to fully clean and rinse out any plastic bottle you want to reuse, and be careful when you use up old cleaning supplies. If an accidental mixture occurs, it is very important to remove yourself from the area, ventilate the room as much as possible, and contact local authorities to handle the potentially hazardous situation.

lungs when inhaled. Ammonia is also incredibly dangerous when combined with bleach, a common household accident that can result in a chemical reaction that produces toxic chloramines. In their most benign form, the chemicals can irritate the lungs, throat, eyes, and nasal passages. In stronger forms, they can be downright deadly. Such an accident could occur from something as simple as lathering up with a product that contains ammonia or urea (an ingredient sometimes found in facial and body cleansers, conditioners, and lotions) in a shower recently cleaned with bleach but not thoroughly rinsed. Also, when ammonia gets into the water supply, even in the very diluted form usually used in households, it can be toxic for aquatic animals.

You'll be making great strides toward green cleaning if you first concentrate on ridding your home of the supplies mentioned in the Terrible Ten—specifically ammonia and bleach and any product that contains them. Throughout this book, you'll find replacements suggested for the Terrible Ten, as well as some techniques that will help you avoid needing any of them in the first place.

The Ground Rules

Typically, using hot, soapy water and a little elbow grease can adequately clean most household surfaces. Really! There is almost no need for all those specialized cleaners available for sale. Just plain old soap does the trick (and not the "antibacterial" kind). Nor is there much reason to "disinfect" everything. When you need a little extra scrubbing or acidic power, turn to the environmentally safe products we'll explore in this chapter: baking soda, lemon juice, vinegar, and salt.

But first, some ground rules for green cleaning:

Don't dump it, use it!

If you've just decided to go green with your household cleaning, look before you leap.

THUMBS-UP OR NOT?

There are several environmental organizations that lend their "seal of approval" to green cleaning products. Of course, whether a manufacturer seeks their approval is entirely voluntary. You may wish to investigate these organizations and their standards, and perhaps opt for those products with certification. Check out Web sites such as the Green Guide, www.thegreenguide.com, for more information.

Experts suggest the best way for you to get rid of a product that you no longer want is, well, to use it up. After all, whether you finish using the product or throw it away, it all has to end up somewhere. If you just can't use the stuff, give it to someone who will. If you must, call your local landfill or recycling center and ask how to best dispose of it.

Many communities have annual or semiannual household hazardous waste days, where residents can take the items not usually permitted in the trash (or that shouldn't go into the trash at all) to the department of public works, dump, or recycling center. If your community offers this sort of program, take advantage of it—what a great opportunity to rid your house of any unused "traditional" cleaners, especially the ones that you haven't used in a while or have only used once. You know the ones—they're way in the back of the cabinets under your sinks, collecting a layer of dust, because you haven't touched them since "that spill" or "that project."

To find out if your area offers such a program, check your community's Web site, or that of a neighboring community, as some cities or towns will share such programs with surrounding areas. Check page 157 for a list of more resources to consider.

Read before you buy

How's a person supposed to know what is in those cleaning products, or know what's good and what's bad? Well, the truth is, you often don't. Hazardous products have to be labeled as such, but the manufacturers are not required to reveal every

CLEANING CONUNDRUM

PAPER TOWEL, DISHRAG, OR SPONGE?
The debate rages on as to whether paper towels, dishrags, or sponges are the most effective for cleaning. It'll be up to you to decide which to use based on your preference, but you should also consider environmental factors.

While paper towels will break down in a landfill, they certainly use up a lot of paper and are probably the most wasteful. Sponges can be made from petroleum products, but you may be able to find some natural sponges that are biodegradable. Of course, dishrags are cloth and thus easily reused. There is some worry that rags and sponges harbor germs and bacteria, but these items can be easily washed in the washing machine. You can also clip sponges to your dishwasher racks for a good rinsing. Thankfully, many newer dishwasher models not only have a "sanitize" feature, but are in compliance with governmental ratings for energy efficiency.

ingredient in them. This applies to green cleaning products as well. Although a bottle of cleaner may be marked "earth-friendly," you still won't know exactly what it's comprised of unless that particular company has chosen to tell you. Here's an example label from an alleged green cleaning product. While the list of what *isn't* in this product is impressive, the label still manages to avoid telling you what *is* inside:

Green Product X is *"eco-friendly and biodegradable; clear of dyes and fragrance free; not harmful to those with allergies or other chemical sensitivities; no preservatives; not harmful to wildlife or plant life; not harmful to rivers and streams; no animal testing and no animal ingredients; contains no EPA priority pollutants; contains no phosphate, chlorine, ammonia, sodium lauryl sulfate or sodium laureth sulfate, or diethanolamine."*

Whew! The label may give us some idea about which ingredients we may not want to have in something we buy, but it doesn't say anything about what the product actually contains. A good rule of thumb to follow is that if the product you're considering doesn't give you a list of ingredients and instructions for how to use the product, don't buy it. You should demand the same level of disclosure with "earth-friendly" products as with anything else you buy. Words to watch out for on the label include: *poison, danger, warning,* or *caution.* And don't be fooled if a label says "nontoxic"; scientifically speaking, it's a term that doesn't really mean anything.

Actually, to decipher the label-reading mumbo jumbo even further, what "nontoxic" does mean is that by the standards set forth by the Food and Drug Administration (FDA) and by the Consumer Product Safety Commission, the ingredients have not been found to pose a significant health risk or are in concentrations lower than the threshold set forth for known human carcinogens and other known toxins.

Buy the minimum of what you need

After considering the ingredients and how useful the product will be to you, you should carefully calculate how much of it you're likely to use. You don't have to buy a gallon of something if you only need to use it once, or if you have not tried it before. More often than not, if you don't like it or it doesn't work, waste will be the result. If you can't buy a small quantity of the product, search for something else.

Buy in bulk

This is an alternative to buying in small quantities. Buy the largest quantity you can of the ingredients you will be using the most. Then transfer those bulk items to smaller containers, placing them in strategic locations throughout your house—for example, under the kitchen sink and in the laundry room. There's no need to go out and buy spiffy new containers. You may have already been collecting (perhaps accidentally) old spray bottles, canisters, and plastic containers. Now's your chance to use them! For instance, one friend dug out her collection of very outdated canisters and measuring cups from her college years to hold and scoop her various supplies of baking soda. Remember, the green cleaner likes to reuse.

Buy a multipurpose cleaner

Of course, if you take the DIY cleaning advice given throughout this book—we'll introduce you to the many uses of baking soda, lemons and lemon juice, salt, and vinegar in a moment—you've already covered all of your bases. But if you still must buy a commercial cleaner, as a rule, buying a multipurpose cleaner is better than buying many single-purpose items.

Avoid aerosol sprays

Long before we worried about global warming, we worried about a hole in the ozone layer. Back in the 1970s, a big environmental win was the banning of chlorofluorocarbons (CFCs) in aerosol sprays, which were believed responsible for depleting the ozone layer protecting us from the sun. It's also wise to consider that if you're spraying, say, an air freshener throughout your home, you're going to be breathing in some of it. This is another area where "better safe than sorry" might be the best rule. Instead, opt for liquid, paste, or powder forms.

TOOL TIP   A NEW TWIST ON TOWELS

When hand towels reach a point where they appear permanently soiled, treat yourself to new towels and use the old ones as cleaning cloths. Terry cloth rags will pick up stray hair better than smooth rags or paper towels, and they are better for polishing glass, mirrors, and chrome.

Makes scents

If you're stuck on having scented air, realize too that in most cases, many sprays only mask odors and don't actually remove them. Essential oils and soy candles are a great, greener way to freshen your space. Try using several drops of lavender, ylang-ylang, cinnamon, clove, peppermint, true vanilla or patchouli oils—and even a well-placed coffee bean or two— on a heated lamp ring, doused over a bowl of potpourri, or in a spray of witch hazel for an effect that will leave your home smelling nice.

Using lavender will also help disinfect, as it has antibacterial and anti-pest qualities. Peppermint and clove oils are also natural pest deterrents, as is natural cedar. Find out more about using essential oils on page 111. Of course, it is important to make sure that neither you nor your family members are allergic to any essential oils. And just as with any substance, special care and precautions must be taken when using near, on, or around children, babies, pregnant women, and nursing mothers. Remember, while natural may be safer, not all natural methods are always safe for everyone.

Don't get crazy

You may be totally sold on the idea of greening up your home and the planet, but don't get too fervent—you'll just end up annoying your family and friends. Instead, concentrate on doing what you can. Don't beat yourself up if you actually use ammonia now and then, or stoop to buy some disposable cleaning wipes. Do your part, yes, but try to keep everything in perspective.

Build Your Own Green Cleaning Kit

Now it's time to look at the products you *should* be using: baking soda, vinegar, lemon juice, and salt. These four, combined with elbow grease, hot water, and sometimes a few other household ingredients, can give your home plenty of sparkle while being kinder to the planet,

yourself, and your family. We'll call these the **Fantastic Four:**

Baking soda

Baking soda is environmentally benign, or harmless, which explains its longevity and popularity in the cleaning-product world. Baking soda makes an excellent cleaner because it has no odor (in fact it absorbs odors), is mildly abrasive and gentle, and yet it can break down acids, making it great for beating grease and grime. Actually, baking soda is amazingly  versatile. Do some research—you can find many resources on ways to use baking soda. It can even replace many of your

USING THE FANTASTIC FOUR

The rest of this book is devoted to showing how you can best use these top four cleaning ingredients. Generally, you'll find three different ways the ingredients can be used for effective cleaning:

Paste: When a tip or recipe asks you to make a paste, it means mix a dry ingredient with just enough of a liquid ingredient to get a mixture with the consistency of toothpaste. Measurements are not important; you should be able to apply the mixture on a vertical surface and not have it drip off immediately.

Solution: Use 4 tablespoons for each quart of warm water, or the equivalent ratio for smaller jobs. Follow the directions carefully.

Direct application: Lightly apply to a damp sponge or directly onto the area to be cleaned. There should be no dilution.

less earth-friendly personal care products, from toothpaste and deodorant to a fizzy antacid to help with indigestion.

Vinegar

Vinegar is abundant, inexpensive, and not harmful to the environment or human beings. It also happens to have two great cleaning characteristics: It's acidic and it can act as a disinfectant. Use distilled white vinegar in the suggestions throughout this book unless otherwise indicated.

Lemons and lemon juice

Keep a bottle of lemon juice and a few lemons on hand to lend

a pleasant smell to your new green cleaning techniques. Lemons have antibacterial and antiseptic qualities much like those of vinegar, and their acidic qualities make them ideal for getting out stains. Besides, a fresh lemon scent just seems to cheer people up!

Salt

Salt has wonderfully mild abrasive qualities, plus it works very well at absorbing liquids. Next time

Vim 'n' Vinegar

1 teaspoon baking soda

2 teaspoons vinegar or lemon juice

1/4 teaspoon liquid dish soap

2 cups hot water

Baking Soda Blast

16 ounces baking soda

4 tablespoons liquid dish soap

1 cup warm water

Lemon-Scented Spray

1/2 cup water

1/4 cup vinegar

1/4 cup lemon juice

you drop a raw egg on the floor, cover it with salt and let it sit awhile—you'll see what I mean. In the cleaning suggestions, use regular table salt unless otherwise noted.

The Power of the Pump

Every household needs a good all-purpose cleaner. If you're buying the Fantastic Four in bulk, you'll always have the ingredients on hand for making the cleaners listed on the opposite page. Mix them up as needed; you'll be making far fewer trips down the cleaning products aisle of your grocery store.

Multipurpose cleaner

Just one of our homemade mixtures listed can probably replace a lot of the commercial cleaners you may have around your home. Try the three multipurpose cleaner variations listed and determine which one seems to work the best for you.

Eco-facts

On average, Americans consume products twice as much as they did 50 years ago!

Eco-facts

Paper and cardboard make up over a third of U.S. landfills.

First, start with a spray bottle (you may already have one among your cleaning supplies). Use up whatever's inside, and then give the bottle a good rinse with hot, soapy water. Then simply fill it with one of our green cleaning recipes. Be sure to mix well and label appropriately. And while you've given your old containers a good rinse, don't forget about the regular and foaming pump containers.

Note: Don't keep and reuse any containers from cleaners marked "poison" or "hazardous." Those containers need to be rinsed and disposed of properly. In some cases, a thorough cleaning of the container should be done by professionals trained to work with hazardous materials in a regulated area. In other words, now is not the time to reuse the container from the toilet bowl cleaner. While the green cleaner loves to reuse and recycle, you have to know how to choose your battles— and your bottles!

The skinny on dishwashing liquid

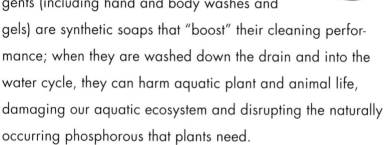

It's a staple in our homes—the ever-present dishwashing liquid, foam, or gel—but unless the one you're using is phosphate free, you're harming both your family and the environment. Liquid detergents (including hand and body washes and gels) are synthetic soaps that "boost" their cleaning performance; when they are washed down the drain and into the water cycle, they can harm aquatic plant and animal life, damaging our aquatic ecosystem and disrupting the naturally occurring phosphorous that plants need.

The most eco-friendly soap to use is, well, soap, in either bar or cake form. But even these might be altered with phosphates to enhance their extra sudsing and foaming powers.

Eco-facts

According to the Web site Treehugger, there are 17,000 petrochemicals available for home use. Only 30 percent of those have been tested for how they relate to human health and the environment.

When choosing your soap, look for glycerin-based, soy-based, or other plant-derived bar soaps. Using these types also often means less packaging and therefore less waste.

However, if you're stuck on using a liquid soap, don't despair—you can make your own! Start by taking a plastic bottle; preferably, while you're finishing up your old plastic bottles, save one that is close to being empty. Rinse the bottle out completely. Then, cut up a new bar of soap into bits small enough to make it through the mouth of the bottle.

Next, add just enough warm water to the bottle to cover the soap bits and let it sit. Every few days, check on the gelatin forming in the bottle. Add more bits of the solid soap and more water until you reach the consistency you prefer. It's important to remember to stir or swirl the mixture so that the soap and water become more homogenized. Before use, give the bottle a good shake, and voilà, you have your liquid (or gel) cleanser. This works for both dish soap and body washes. If you want foam instead of liquid or a gel, save the bottles from the foams that you already use—it's the type of pump on the bottle (and not the substance inside the bottle) that makes the foaming action.

Go Green at the Grocery

Give yourself a pat on the back if you're already among those who just say no to the ubiquitous plastic shopping bag and take your own bag with you instead. If you're really making a green commit-ment, use bags that are 100-percent organic fair trade cotton and are made from sustainable practices. Plastic bags land in the oceans, where sea turtles often mistake them for jellyfish, ingest them, and suffocate. Plastic bags also become airborne and end up in trees, gutters, and sewer systems. They do not break down by decomposing; instead, they break down by being exposed to light. When they finally do break down, they simply become smaller bits of plastic-based chemicals. Buried in landfills, the bags and pieces last for generations. Experts say less than 1 percent of plastic bags are recycled.

Eco-facts

Plastic bags are among the most common items of debris found in coastal cleanups.

To make your shopping a little greener, BYOB—Bring Your Own Bags (many grocery stores also sell reusable bags). However, if you still get plastic bags, reuse them—they make great book bags when going to the library, or they can be used as trash bags to stow in your car. Reusable plastic bags also work well as receptacles for used kitty litter or for picking up after your dog. Just remember to dispose of the animal refuse properly.

Junk the Junk Mail!

For most people, every trip to the mailbox results in another trip to the recycling bin. Often three-quarters of our daily mail is stuff we didn't ask for and don't want. It's an annoyance, but junk mail also doesn't do the environment any good: According to the WildWest Institute, a Montana-based environmental organization, approximately 100 million trees are used each year to produce junk mail. Another 28 billion gallons of water might be used in turning those trees into paper. It really seems silly and wasteful, especially considering that most junk mail is tossed directly into the garbage. The response rate to junk mail is less than 2 percent!

There are services that allow you to remove yourself from direct-mail marketing lists. These services are provided by the companies who build and supply lists to marketers, offering consumers a chance to get off some lists and put themselves on others, or remove themselves entirely. Here are three organizations to look into:

- DMA Mail Preference Services, www.dmachoice.org
- Catalog Choice, www.catalogchoice.org
- OptOutPrescreen (handles only credit and insurance offers), www.optoutprescreen.com or 1-888-567-8688

KITCHEN CATCHALLS

According to the sensationalist media, our kitchens are about to kill us. Salmonella, E. coli, garden-variety germs—there's all sorts of nastiness lurking everywhere, just waiting to pounce, right? Wrong. You do not need to cave in to this kind of fear by adopting an around-the-clock habit of cleaning and disinfecting everything. Reasonable daily care and attention, using some very basic cleaning ingredients, can make your kitchen as clean and shiny as it needs to be. And because you're using fewer harsh cleaners and disinfectants, the earth will thank you as well. Remember, less is more.

The best way to stock your green cleaning kit is with an economy-size box of baking soda, a gallon jug of vinegar, and some basic table salt in as large a quantity as you can find. Baking soda is an excellent green cleaning product to use throughout your home, especially in the kitchen. It's also food-safe and has no odor. Baking soda is mildly abrasive, yet it can't harm your surfaces, whether they're linoleum or expensive imported Italian marble.

You may also want to keep lemons and lemon juice around for some of the tasks described below. Vinegar and lemon can often serve the same purpose, but lemon has a much nicer scent.

It's time to roll up those sleeves and get started! We'll tackle the sink first.

Sink Drains

First, a lesson in what *not* to use. As mentioned earlier, one of the more caustic products you may have in your home is a commercial drain cleaner designed to unclog sinks. If you've ever had a clogged sink, you've probably used one of these incredibly corrosive cleaners. The typical acidic drain cleaner essentially burns the gunk in your pipes, clearing it away.

Some drain cleaners are now designed to use enzyme action, which may sound better than acid, but enzymes can gradually eat away at your pipes. Injecting air or carbon dioxide into

---

CLEANING CONUNDRUM **THE DISINFECTANT DILEMMA**

Washing your hands with antibacterial soaps and cleaning the house with disinfectant wipes—seems like a no-brainer, right? Actually, the substances that make soap and other products antibacterial and allow them to "disinfect" are herbicides, pesticides, and fungicides that help eliminate odor-causing bacteria and microbes. The Environmental Protection Agency classifies 275 of the antibacterial elements in cleansers as pesticides because they kill microbes. Some, such as triclosan, trigger production of a probable carcinogenic chloroform.

In fact, some of the "active ingredients" in antibacterial products have been linked to a variety of serious health problems including liver, kidney, and digestive damage; behavioral problems in children; damage to the nervous system; and brain development and reproductive defects. Even more, overuse of these products can impair the body's ability to fight off common infections and viruses.

Instead of antibacterial soaps and wipes, opt for natural germ-fighters such as vinegar, baking soda, and lavender oil in either a solution, suspended in an inert oil such as mineral or apricot oil, or by direct application.

the drain is less harmful, so you might look for those products instead. Another approach is to use high-pressure water treatments. Still, quite often pouring a lot of boiling water down the drain will do the trick. Try that process first before moving on to the more advanced methods.

Once you've cleared a nasty clog, commit yourself to practicing preventative maintenance in your kitchen sink. For starters, make sure that nothing solid goes down the drain, especially if you do not have a garbage disposal. Keep a small compost bin or bucket next to the faucet to remind you to scrape those plates clean before putting them in the sink or dishwasher. Once a week, dump ¼ cup baking soda down each of your kitchen drains, followed by ½ cup vinegar. Let this mixture sit in the drain for 20 minutes or more without any other liquids going down. While this is sitting, boil some water on the stove. Finally, flush the drains with the boiling water.

You might need to give the process some added *oomph* if a lot of greasy plates have been rinsed recently. If that's the case, mix ½ cup salt and ½ cup baking soda together, pour down the drain, and then flush with hot tap water.

Ovens

Again, another household cleaning product no-no is the aerosol oven cleaner. It's so strong that the product's instructions practically scream, "Open all windows and doors, spray the stuff into your oven, grab the children, and run for your lives!"

Let's take that as a clue that perhaps you should use something different.

Self-cleaning ovens are a miracle of modern science—if you have the technology, good for you. However, if you don't have an oven equipped with that feature (or yours has just given up), try not to reach for the can of spray-on oven cleaner.

To clean an oven manually, sprinkle about a ¼-inch layer of baking soda over the entire bottom of the oven. Use a clean spray bottle to wet the baking soda with water. Over the next few hours, spray the baking soda every so often to keep it moist. Then let the baking soda mixture sit overnight. In the morning, scrape and scoop the dried baking soda and grime out of the oven with a damp sponge. Rinse the residue off.

As with your kitchen sink, the best way to tackle interior oven cleaning is with preventative main-tenance. Keeping up with the grease and grime a little bit at a time will mean you don't have to do a big cleaning event very often.

After you've done a major cleaning, finish the job by using a sponge to wipe down the entire surface with a mixture of half vinegar and half water. This will help prevent grease buildup. Be sure to give the entire interior a wipe once each week with a sponge soaked in pure vinegar.

Another preventative trick is to cover the bottom of your oven with aluminum foil when you're baking something that may overflow—a blueberry pie, say, or perhaps an overstuffed lasagna. If something does accidentally spill inside and onto the unprotected bottom of the oven, as soon as it is safely pos-sible (make sure the oven isn't hot!), cover the mess with salt

Eco-facts

According to the Natural Resources Defense Council, one leaky faucet can waste up to 20 gallons of water per day. A leaky toilet can waste up to 200 gallons per day!

and let it stand. It should become hard and crisp enough for you to lift off the surface of the cold oven with a plastic spatula or some other item that won't scratch the interior.

If you have vents above your oven, you should be checking them about every six months for grease buildup. To clean, wipe the vents with a sponge soaked in pure vinegar. Use an old toothbrush dipped in vinegar to get at the grime that may have built up in small crevices or other hard-to-reach places. If the filter is metal and removable, give it a soak in a vinegar solution.

Now that you've tackled some of the hardest jobs in your home, let's take a greener look at some more everyday kitchen cleanups.

Stovetops

Spills on the stovetop can be easily cleaned if sprinkled with salt first. The salt acts as an absorbent, plus it has a mild abrasive quality that won't harm the surface. If you've spilled something into your burner pans on your electric stove, sprinkle the spill with salt and cinnamon, and wipe away. The cinnamon will mask the burned-on smell the next time you use the burner.

All stovetops, even ceramic glass ones, can be cleaned easily with a baking soda solution. Use a toothbrush dipped in baking soda to get into any tight corners. Then rinse everything very thoroughly to avoid leaving a white residue.

Microwaves

Now, some of us have a natural talent for exploding things in the microwave—usually involving some kind of red sauce that stains. To easily get rid of this type of spatter or greasy buildup, add ¼ cup vinegar to 1 cup water in a glass measuring cup. Boil the mixture for three minutes in the microwave. But don't open the door just yet—let it stand in the microwave for about ten more minutes. Soon, everything should be loosened up nicely.

Wipe the entire inside of the microwave clean with a damp sponge or soft cloth. Wipe from top to bottom and collect anything that falls to the floor of the microwave, tossing it into your compost bin.

TOOL TIP   **BOIL AND BUBBLE**

Boiling vinegar in the microwave is a good way to rid it (and your home) of that persistent burned-popcorn smell.

Lemons also may be used as a variation. Heat a bowl of water with lemon slices in your microwave for 30 to 60 seconds, then wipe out the oven. Stains will be easier to remove and old food odors will be neutralized.

Remember to use microwave-safe containers when nuking your food. Many plastics and even paper towels break down when microwaved, releasing toxins that leach into food.

Utensils and Containers

Since baking soda absorbs oil, anything that has an oily residue, such as a salad dressing cruet, can easily be cleaned by shaking a bit of baking soda inside, then rinsing with warm water.

Plastic, silicone, and rubber kitchen utensils are easily stained. To remove these marks, make a baking soda paste and apply it to the stained areas using a scouring pad, sponge, or rag. Similarly, if you have stained plastic food containers for storing leftovers, use the same method. You can make the baking soda paste out of water or lemon juice, which will add a clean, fresh scent.

If you have a thermos or lunchbox that is beginning to smell a little funky, pour ¼ cup salt into it and close it up for the night. In the morning, rinse and wipe clean, and it should smell fresh again.

Wood and Wooden Things

Clean a wooden cutting board with soap and a little water. Follow this by wiping it with a damp cloth dipped in salt. The salt will give the wood a new look and a fresh feeling. Similarly, you should wipe your wooden cutting board, breadbox, or salad bowls now and then with a sponge dipped in

---

LEFT THE COOKIES IN THE OVEN TOO LONG?

Covering a cookie sheet in baking soda and hot water and allowing it to soak can remove burned-on stains. After the soak, scrub with baking soda applied directly on a sponge, rag, or scrubber. Other aluminum pans can take on a rather grungy look after years of use as well. Remove stains by boiling the soiled pans on a stovetop inside other pans large enough to hold them. Add 2 tablespoons vinegar to enough water to cover, then just let them boil.

vinegar; it removes any grime and odor buildup, since wood tends to harbor grease and odors. A baking soda solution can also be used for this purpose. Another great cutting board cleaner is lemon juice. Just rub some into the cutting board and leave it overnight. In the morning, rinse thoroughly.

When your wooden utensils or cutting boards start to fade, crack, or become brittle, don't throw them out. Instead, apply a generous amount of olive oil onto them and rub it into the wood, following its grain. Depending upon how dry and cracked they are, it may take two or three applications to return them to a healthier state. If any oil seems to "pool," or if the utensils or cutting boards are still very oily to the touch even after letting them sit for a while, gently dab up the excess with an absorbent, lint-free cloth.

Pots, Pans, Cookware, and Dishes

While some of today's high-end enamel cookware shouldn't be cleaned with abrasives, it is fine to apply a baking soda paste to tough areas, then scrub to clear. A casserole dish with stubborn, baked-on food can be cleansed

CLEANING CONUNDRUM **DISHWASHER VS. HAND WASHING**

Have you ever wondered whether it saves more water and energy to wash your dishes by hand than to run a dishwasher? Well, some smart folks at the University of Bonn in Germany have done the math. The winner: the dishwasher. A well-operating dishwasher uses half the energy and one-sixth of the water you would use when hand washing, and it uses less soap. Plus, the dishes get cleaner in the machine.

---

by adding boiling water and about 3 tablespoons salt. Let it stand until the water cools, then clean as usual.

Roasting pans and broiler pans can be among the most difficult to get clean. Often they won't fit into the dishwasher; even when they do, the machine still doesn't do a good job getting them clean. A way to avoid multiple cleanings and save time is to fill or cover the pan with very hot water and just let it sit. If more drastic measures need to be taken, fill the pan with water and boil it on your stovetop for a few minutes. Then wipe clean or scrub with some salt sprinkled onto a sponge. For the toughest spots, sprinkle salt directly onto the problem areas and scrub.

One of the best ways to clean a really messy broiler pan is to set it on the stove while the pan is still hot and fill the lower drip pan with very hot water. Then place the slotted upper pan on top and cover that with paper towels. The hot water underneath produces a steam that helps loosen the grime. The paper towels do their part by absorbing the grime or keeping it damp. After a half hour or so, the remains will be easy to wipe away, or at least a little easier to scrub off with a scouring pad. Finally, sprinkle the entire surface with baking soda and give it a good once-over.

Speaking of grease, you can clean a gritty frying pan by simmering it on the stovetop with ¼ inch water and ½ cup vinegar for about ten minutes. Afterward, wash as usual.

Clay pots used in cooking also become stained or take on odors. To solve this problem, fill such a pot with water and add 1 to 4 tablespoons baking soda. Let the mixture stand for a half hour or more, then rinse and dry thoroughly. Sometimes

---

CREAM OF TARTAR

Cream of tartar shows up now and then in recipes for foods such as meringue, but it also serves another purpose. As a mild acid, it can be useful for a number of cleaning projects, including taking stains out of white clothing. Try it on a spot of rust by making a paste mixed with water and applying it to the rust. Allow it to sit for a while, then rinse thoroughly.

a clay cooker can start to grow spots of mold. Brush the mold with a paste made of baking soda and water and let it stand. If you can, give it an extra boost by putting the cooker into direct sunlight. After half an hour, brush the paste away and rinse the pot.

If your copper-bottom pans and kettles need sprucing up, don't turn to toxic polishes. Polishes are high on the list of products to avoid; instead, toss the toxins and take up your salt and lemon juice. Copper-bottom pans and kettles can be made shiny again with a paste made of salt and lemon juice. Rub the paste in with a cloth, then wipe and rinse thoroughly.

You can also clean copper-bottom pans with a similar paste treatment substituting vinegar for the lemon juice. Or, if you like, try filling a spray bottle with undiluted vinegar and spraying it directly onto the bottoms of the pans. Let it sit for a bit, and you should see the tarnish begin to evaporate. Then sprinkle with salt, scrub, and rinse. For really tough stains, coarse salt (such as sea salt or kosher salt) works better than table salt. Another method is to simply cut a lemon in half, dip it in (or sprinkle onto it) some salt to cover the meat of the fruit, and rub in circular motions onto the copper. Afterward, rinse and dry thoroughly.

Fine China and Crystal

If you have fine crystal that needs cleaning, add a cup of vinegar to a sink full of warm water, wash carefully, rinse, and dry. This should get rid of any spots or streaks.

Remove stains from china with a paste of vinegar and salt; apply the paste and let it sit for a while, then rinse off. You can also use a paste of baking soda and water, or make a paste by mixing powdered automatic dishwashing detergent and water.

Tool Tip   TEACH OLD TOOLS NEW TRICKS

When you're done with your kitchen cleaning, consider ways you can make your tools last longer. You can renew old sponges, nylon scrubbers, and scrub brushes by soaking them overnight in a solution of 4 tablespoons baking soda mixed with 1 cup water. Baking soda has the effect of softening stiff brushes and sponges, and it will remove odors as well. Mops and cleaning rags can be treated the same way; soaking them in a baking soda solution gets rid of bad smells and residues.

Surface Cleaning

Wipe your kitchen countertops with undiluted vinegar once a day—they'll shine and keep the kitchen smelling fresh. You can also cut a lemon in half, sprinkle it with baking soda, and scrub the countertop to achieve the same thing. Mind you, this would take quite an investment in lemons if you were to do it daily, but this trick works on any kitchen surface that needs cleaning, whether it is a counter, dish, or stove.

Cleaning the stainless steel sink can be a satisfying task to undertake. By week's end, the sink can look a little grimy, so it's best to clear everything out and away before starting the job. Then just sprinkle baking soda onto a sponge and go to it. Around the faucets and knobs, use a toothbrush dipped in baking soda. As long as you remember to rinse thoroughly, everything will turn out shiny—baking soda can leave behind a harmless white residue if you don't get it all off immediately.

Any stainless steel surface in the kitchen will benefit from this treatment. Lemon juice is also good for any soap scum or hard water deposits around your sink.

If you have a white porcelain sink, a combination of baking soda and vinegar on a sponge does a great job on minor stains. Porcelain stains very easily, so it's best to tackle any problem spots immediately.

If you have tile and grout in your kitchen, treat them regularly with undiluted vinegar on a sponge to cut the inevitable greasy buildup. Scrub stains with vinegar and allow to dry. Afterward, rub the vinegar off with a dry rag. For added strength, try tackling the stains by scrubbing them with a toothbrush dipped in a paste of baking soda and water. Afterward, rinse off.

Every so often, laminate countertops can get stained with something that seems unremovable, such as blueberry juice, tomato sauce, or red wine. Diligently apply a baking soda paste to the spot and allow it to sit until dry. Then rub the paste off with a dry towel and the stain should disappear. Such stains can also often be removed by applying straight lemon juice. Scrub, then rinse clean.

Eco-facts

It takes 95 percent more energy to create a brand-new aluminum can than to make a can from recycled aluminum.

Floors

Tile floors can best be cleaned with a bucket of warm water and ½ cup baking soda. Just mop using the mixture and rinse thoroughly. Add lemon juice to the water to create a fresh scent. Use baking soda on a damp sponge to remove those black heel marks that spring up when you least expect them.

If your kitchen floor is ceramic, mop it with a gallon of warm water mixed with 1 cup vinegar. Rinsing is not necessary. Linoleum and vinyl floors can be cleaned with the same mixture. If you need a little extra polish, mop the entire floor with club soda.

Tea and Coffee Stains

Coffee and tea stains can be removed from light-colored cups and mugs by using a damp sponge dipped in baking soda. If the spots are proving stubborn, try rubbing them with a bit of salt.

TOOL TIP — **SHAKE IT UP**

The next time you use up a shaker can of Parmesan cheese or some similar product, clean the can and let it dry. Then fill it from your supply of baking soda. Keep the can top flipped open and put it in your refrigerator to let it do double duty—the baking soda will deodorize your fridge as well as be handy when you need to grab some for a cleaning project. On a side note, the next time you go to the grocery store, skip the can of processed cheese and opt for a fresh block of Parmesan instead. You can grate what you need from the block each time. This will help you reduce waste and avoid some of the less healthy preservatives found in commercially processed foods.

If you have rust and mineral deposits on a teapot or an old stovetop-style coffee percolator, they can be removed by filling the pot with water and adding 2 tablespoons baking soda and the juice from half a lemon. Gently boil for 15 minutes, then rinse thoroughly. If you want to get coffee and mineral stains out of the glass or stainless steel pot of your coffeemaker, try this variation: Add 1 cup crushed ice, 1 tablespoon water, and 4 teaspoons salt to the pot when it is cold, swish around, and then wash as usual. Again, for really stubborn stains, substitute regular table salt with coarse salt.

Many of these methods can also be used for cleaning blenders and food processors. The baking soda will help get rid of any lingering odors from foods like peppers or garlic, and the salt and ice will help clean the blades as they "chew" them up. Rinse the blades thoroughly and let them dry, or run through the dishwasher if necessary (and if possible).

Silverware

If you'll remember, polish is on our list of the Terrible Ten. Here's a more eco-friendly polish that will take the tarnish off of Grandma's silverware: Pour a little salt onto a soft cloth and gently rub the pieces. Then wash the silverware by hand with dish soap and warm water. Carefully dry each piece. Sterling silver can be cleaned with a paste of 2 tablespoons salt and ½ cup vinegar. Gently rub in the paste, then rinse and dry thoroughly. You can also substitute cream of tartar for the salt in this method.

Garbage Pails and Disposals

Keep your kitchen garbage pail smelling fresher by sprinkling a bit of baking soda in the bottom each time you empty it.

Every now and then, wash and deodorize the can with a solution of baking soda in warm water.

It's also a good idea to give your garbage disposal the royal treatment every month or so. Pour ¼ cup each salt, baking soda, and dishwasher detergent into the disposal, turn on the hot water, and run the disposal. Doing this should clean out the gunk and get rid of lingering odors. You can also drop the rind from a citrus fruit such as a lemon, lime, or grapefruit down the disposal. Grind away—the rind helps to clean the disposal's "teeth" and gives a fresh scent to your kitchen.

Refrigerators

You may already know to deodorize your fridge with a box of baking soda, but don't forget that you can also sprinkle some onto a damp sponge and use it to clean your fridge's interior surfaces. Add equal parts

baking soda and salt if you need a little scrubbing action on spills and drips. For a deodorization variation, try storing half a lemon in an open container inside the refrigerator.

Do the cubes that are coming out of the automatic ice cube maker taste a little unpleasant? Try cleaning the removable parts of the unit with baking soda and water.

De-dirt Your Fruit

Worrying about what pesticides or other chemical residues may be lingering on fresh fruits and veggies? Scrubbing your produce with a little bit of baking soda can remove residues and dirt. Rinse everything well and be sure to dry the produce to ensure maximum shelf life—leaving fresh foods damp will make them deteriorate more quickly.

Salt can help remove the gritty dirt that can sometimes hide stubbornly in your lettuce, spinach, or leeks. Place the vegetables in a bowl of lukewarm water, add 1 tablespoon salt, swish it around a little, and let soak 20 to 30 minutes. Rinse thoroughly in a colander.

Let It Soak

Most messes in the kitchen can be more easily cleaned if you let the pot, pan, rack, or whatnot soak in some hot water. If you're using a cleaning product, apply it to the item first and then let it sit. This avoids using too much cleaning product at any one time, and it can also save you some elbow grease.

BATHROOM BUFF-UPS

The bathroom is a place where your primary cleaning MO might be about controlling germs, and rightly so. But again, diligence and a reasonable amount of care will keep your bathroom sanitary and sparkly without having to bring in the heavy guns—disinfectants.

The process of disinfecting something is to destroy microorganisms living on it. The problem is, the products that disinfect are often hazardous. We know you want to be sure your bathrooms are free of microbes; after all, some of them can cause illnesses. But don't panic. The fact is, germs and microbes are everywhere, and they'll be there whether you clean them out or not. You may toil and scrub, but they always come back. It's just a part of life.

Enough talk, let's move into action! Now, to counteract these daily foes, we must focus on keeping our living spaces and ourselves at least moderately clean. For everyday cleaning in the bathroom, use baking soda liberally. Just sprinkle it on a damp sponge and wipe off dirty surfaces.

Shower and Sink Drains

Just as with your kitchen sink, you should practice preventative maintenance with your bathroom sink and shower. Once a week, lift the drain cover in your tub and use a cotton swab to remove the hair that has accumulated there. Then pour ½ cup  baking soda followed by 1 cup vinegar down the drain. Let this sit for 20 minutes, then flush the drain with very hot water. To help keep your tub drain unclogged, buy a plastic or rubber hair strainer; simply place it over your drain and let it do the icky work for you.

If your sink or shower has developed hard-water or mineral deposits, you can get rid of them by soaking paper towels in undiluted vinegar and placing the towels over the stained areas. Let them sit for one hour and then wipe the areas with a damp sponge.

Tubs and Shower Walls

If your tub or shower is made of fiber-
glass, clean it by wiping on a paste of
baking soda and dishwashing liquid
with a sponge. Also, the same paste will
attack hard-water and rust stains on ceramic tile. Use a nylon
scrubber to clean it, then rinse.

Spraying the corners of your tub or your shower doors
and walls with vinegar can loosen built-up soap scum. After
spraying, allow it to dry. Then simply spray it down again
and wipe clean.

Porcelain tubs and sinks can be among the trickiest for
stain removal. Have you ever accidentally spilled an entire
bottle of shampoo into your white tub and unwittingly let the
mess sit there all day? That can certainly clean things up, but

Eco-facts

Do the math: If a family of four uses a low-
flow showerhead in their shower instead of a
full-flow model, they could save approximately
20,000 gallons of water per year.

> **DON'T PLAY RING AROUND THE TUB!**
>
> If you add 2 tablespoons baking soda to your bathwater, you'll avoid creating the dreaded "ring around the tub" effect as well as save yourself cleaning time. Baking soda also has a surprising skin-softening effect!

it's not really the recommended method. Instead, pour lemon juice over the stains, then sprinkle on alum powder (usually available in the spice aisle of the grocery store) and thoroughly work into the stain. If the stain doesn't come out immediately, let the mixture sit on the stain as long as overnight. The next morning, add more lemon juice, scrub again, and rinse.

Nonskid strips or appliqués on your shower or tub floor can easily get stained and are often hard to remove. To clean, dampen the appliqués and sprinkle baking soda directly onto them. Let this sit for 20 minutes and then scrub and rinse. You can remove the appliqués completely by saturating each decal with vinegar to loosen the glue. (For even better results, warm the vinegar in a microwave or on the stove for about three minutes.) Let the vinegar sit for a few minutes, then peel off the

decals. You should be able to remove any leftover glue with a damp sponge.

A bathtub ring requires a strong solvent. Try
soaking paper towels or your reusable cleaning cloths with undiluted vinegar and placing
them on the ring. Let the paper towels or cloths
dry out. Afterward, spray the areas again with
vinegar, then scrub with a sponge.

Grout

Use a baking soda paste to remove mildew stains on the grout
around your tub or shower. Apply the paste and then scrub
it with an old toothbrush until the stain is gone. Remember to
rinse the area well.

Tool Tip   **BE PREPARED**

It's also a good idea to keep a bottle of the
Baking Soda Blast multipurpose cleaner in your bathroom
(see recipe on page 26), ready for use.

Shower Curtains

Clean your shower curtain by sprinkling baking soda on a sponge and
scrubbing. Rinse well. A mildew stain
on the curtain can be tackled by briskly
rubbing in a baking soda and water
paste. When a shower curtain *really*
needs help, remove it and wash on
the delicate/cold cycle of your wash-

ing machine, adding vinegar and baking soda as the only
detergent. Add a bath towel to help agitate the grime off. To
prevent mildew from coming back, add another cup of vinegar
to the final rinse cycle.

You can practice preventative maintenance here as well by
keeping a spray bottle of vinegar and water in your shower.

DIY Dandruff Treatment

Mix a few tablespoons fresh lemon juice
with warm olive oil and gently rub into
your scalp. Leave on for 15 minutes
before shampooing out.

Lemon Hair Magic

Use lemon juice on your hair for a natural conditioner that will make your hair shine. Mix the juice of 1 lemon with 1 cup warm water and apply to hair. Wait a few minutes and then rinse. Unless you want blonde streaks, be sure to rinse completely: Exposing your lemon-treated hair to the sun will bleach light-colored hair if not thoroughly rinsed. For those who want this effect but have red or brunette hair, lime juice has the same properties and will bring out red and lighter-brown highlights.

After each shower, spray down the shower curtain or doors to prevent scum and mineral buildup. Another old-fashioned tip for mildew prevention is to soak the curtains in salt water. This can be done right in the bathtub: Fill it with warm water and pour in ½ cup salt as it fills. Drop the curtains right into the tub to soak, then hang up to drip dry.

Toilets

Once a week, you should pour about a half cup vinegar into your toilets and let it sit for 30 minutes. Next, sprinkle baking soda on a toilet bowl brush and scour any remaining stained areas.

Afterward, flush. You can also mix the vinegar and baking soda, swish the bowl, and allow it to sit for 20 minutes before scrubbing clean. If you have stubborn hard-water or rust stains, you can do the same thing, but scrub the surfaces with a bit of steel wool. Of course, never flush steel wool down the toilet. Instead, rinse it thoroughly, set aside to dry, and store it in a container for the next use.

Floors

Clean a bathroom tile or no-wax floor by adding ½ cup baking soda to a bucket of warm water. Mop the floor with this solution and rinse. Adding lemon juice to the water will give it a nice fresh scent.

Trash Cans

Sprinkle baking soda in the bathroom trash can after each time you empty it. This will help with ongoing odor removal.

Air Fresheners

It's possible to keep the bathroom smelling sweet without having to use an overwhelming aerosol air freshener. For a natural and perpetual air freshener, just keep baking soda in a pretty dish on the back of your toilet or on a shelf, and it will do the trick. For a different smell, you could add a spice like cinnamon to the baking soda. Change this mixture every three months.

To help keep unwanted pests at bay, you can also use cedar chips (found at most general purpose or bath and linen stores), lavender oil, or peppermint oil.

Countertops

Clean marble surfaces with a paste made of baking soda and white vinegar. Wipe clean and buff.

Mirrors

Occasionally, scratches in glass and mirrors can become stained. To remove such stains, mix a bit of dry mustard with enough vinegar to make a paste. Work the paste into the scratch and rub it until the stain is gone, then rinse well.

ENERGY TIPS

Here are some resource-saving tips for the bathroom:

- Teach children to shut off the faucet while they brush their teeth. They can run the water when they're finished. This goes for men who shave as well!
- Limit the time spent in the shower. While it may be relaxing to stand under the spray, gallons of water are going down the drain.
- Don't use the toilet as a wastebasket—what a waste of water!
- Got a lot of little kids? Try bathing small children together.
- A little leak can amount to a lot of wasted water. Repair all leaks that you find. One way to detect a leak in the toilet is to add food coloring to the tank water. Don't flush! Let it sit for a half hour; if you see some of the dye in the bowl, then you have a leaky tank.
- Many manufacturers make water-saving devices for the home, and especially the bathroom. Look into such products as faucet aerators, ultra low-flush toilets, and low-flow showerheads.

CLOTHES ENCOUNTERS

Laundry can seem like an endless task. We go through plenty of clothing, bedding, and towels, and it all needs to be cleaned. But even as we finish up this week's load, there's already more accumulating. It's no surprise, then, that after the refrigerator, the washing machine and dryer are typically the leading culprits in terms of high resource usage in the home—especially if they're older models. Add to that the varied laundry products going down the drain, and you're looking at a couple of not-so-green cleaning machines. But there are ways you can continue to use these convenient appliances while still taking care of the earth. This chapter offers a few practical laundry rules for you to follow, including energy-, labor-, and product-saving tips. We'll concentrate again on our list of the Fantastic Four cleaning products, which do a remarkably good job of getting your clothes clean and keeping them that way.

Laundry Rules: Saving Water and Energy

A washing machine uses a large amount of water. And since the water temperature must be at least 80 degrees Fahrenheit to get your laundry good and clean (colder temperatures have a harder time activating the chemicals in the detergents), it also takes quite a bit of energy to heat the water. Standard-size

Eco-facts

According to the USDA Forest Service, if every family in the United States planted a single tree, the annual level of CO_2 in the atmosphere would be reduced by one billion pounds—nearly 5 percent of the CO_2 humans produce every year.

top-loading washers set on a regular cycle and using the highest water-level setting use approximately 40 to 57 gallons of water *per load.* Using all of that water and energy rather negates the idea of living a green life!

With that in mind, here's a list of ways to minimize the amount of resources used with each load of laundry, without having to resort to taking clothes to the stream and beating them on rocks (but, by all means, feel free to do that if you like):

Green laundry habits

- Wash one full load instead of two small ones. If you don't have a full load, wait until you do.
- If you must run a small load, set your water level accordingly.
- Don't overload your washer. Clothes must be able to move freely in the washer in order to get clean.
- When you can, choose a cold-water rinse for your clothes, even if you washed them in warm or hot water. Cold water

rinses out the soap just as well as warm or hot water.

- Never keep your dryer in a cold place, like a garage or damp basement. It will work much less efficiently if it has to work in the cold.

- Check your dryer exhaust vent periodically to make sure it closes tightly. If it's letting in outside air, the dryer is being forced to work too hard. Plus, you might be allowing your household heat to escape.
- Clean the lint filter in your dryer after every load of laundry for maximum air circulation and efficiency.
- Try to do several loads of laundry at once. When you pop a pile of wet clothes in the dryer right after you've finished a previous load, it takes advantage of the leftover heat.

The Nitty-Gritty

Before moving on, let's go back and review our list of the Terrible Ten:

- Drain cleaners
- Oven cleaners
- Toilet cleaners
- Spot removers
- Silver and other metal polishes
- Furniture polishes
- Cleansers and powdered cleaners
- Window cleaners
- Bleach
- Liquid cleaners

Note that detergents are not on our list. That's because the debate about detergents and the various ingredients they contain continues in the public arena. In the mid-1960s, folks noticed that lakes and rivers were getting choked up with too much aquatic plant growth brought on by the various phosphates added to detergents. Phosphates basically help eliminate some of the problems that come along with using soap, including breaking down soapy buildup (think of the ring that can form on a shirt or in a tub).

Phosphates are strong cleaners, but their useful pros have been overshadowed by their ecological cons. Since the early '60s, community organizers have attempted to ban phosphates outright, to limit their use, or to set acceptable standards for

CLEANING CONUNDRUM

SOAP OR DETERGENT?

Many people are now opting for soap instead of detergent when laundering their clothes. But what's the difference?

Actually, using soap goes as far back as the ancient Babylonians, around 2800 B.C. Mixing water, alkali, and cassia oil—voilà!—they created soap, and the world has been cleaner for it ever since.

Soaps and detergents are both *surfactants*. This means that through a process scientific types call "breaking the surface," surfactants lower the surface tension of water, which helps water soak in and spread around. Soaps are made of materials found in nature, like ash and alkali, while detergents are usually made of synthetic materials, including the phosphates and petroleum-based ingredients we've already mentioned. While soaps go way back to the Babylonians, detergents more or less came into vogue during the post–World War II economic boom.

If soap can clean your clothes and is made of "natural" ingredients, is there any green reason not to use it to wash your clothes? Perhaps. Soaps are more difficult to rinse out of fabric, especially in homes that have hard water, whereas clothes washed with detergents are less prone to this problem. Some people also point out that soap in its standard form deteriorates on the closet shelf, while today's detergents are packaged differently and will not deteriorate. Think hard about your laundry needs—can soap do the trick for you?

their use. These efforts have been met with varying levels of success. Phosphates are banned in some areas of the country and are somewhat regulated in others. Still, there is no universal standard for phosphate use in detergents.

What you can do

Generally speaking, detergents are better than they once were, but most are still made from synthetic petrochemicals that come from oil. Some detergents may also have brighteners, dyes, or artificial fragrances that are bad for you, the environment, or both. Many consumers are finding an increasing number of greener laundering alternatives available on the market. But

AVOID LOADS OF LAUNDRY

No matter what method you use to clean your clothing, reducing the number of times you do the wash will help preserve our planet's resources. According to www.greenerchoices.org (an affiliate of *Consumer Reports*), following these two tips will keep your clothes looking fine without having to wash them as often:

- Hang up clothes immediately after you've worn them, give them a day off between wearings, and air them out before returning them to the closet.
- Use a clothing brush or lint brush occasionally to remove surface dust.

remember, no law requires companies, even "good" companies, to disclose all of the ingredients in products—even green ones. Furthermore, no law defines what "natural" or "earth-friendly" means. The best green detergents should be made *without* nonrenewable, petroleum-based chemicals, and they should be biodegradable, plant-derived, and contain no optical brighteners, dyes, or artificial fragrances.

Some companies voluntarily tell you everything that's in their products, helping consumers to make an informed decision. Some also participate in voluntary programs that show they meet certain environmental criteria. Being a responsible consumer means doing a bit of homework, but it's well worth the effort.

Drying the old-fashioned way

Taking the dryer out of the laundry equation is a great way to incorporate a green process into your household.

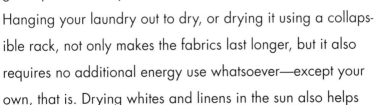

Hanging your laundry out to dry, or drying it using a collapsible rack, not only makes the fabrics last longer, but it also requires no additional energy use whatsoever—except your own, that is. Drying whites and linens in the sun also helps make them brighter, without having to resort to chlorine bleach or alternative whitening agents.

If you find the prospect of hanging laundry out to dry a little daunting, or feel as if you're too busy to try it, try starting

---

CLOTHESLINE CRIMINALS?

Washers and dryers have a lot of effect on the environment since both machines use energy, and, of course, the washer uses quite a bit of water. In fact, household appliance usage accounts for 20 percent of our overall energy use at home, with washers, dryers, and refrigerators at the top of that list. On average, a typical load of laundry in the washing machine costs about 12 cents in energy (at the current, wildly fluctuating oil prices), and drying that same load will cost nearly three times as much.

Hanging your clothes out to dry is far more economical and energy efficient, but the reality is that it's not practical in many parts of the country during the winter months. Air drying indoors is possible, of course—but again, sometimes it's not practical. On the other hand, you might opt for line drying outdoors and not be allowed to do so. Around the country, housing covenants, zoning laws, and landlords sometimes won't allow people to put up a clothesline—usually for aesthetic reasons. But many green-minded residents are fighting back. Read more about it at Project Laundry List, www.laundrylist.org.

small. Perhaps begin with air drying fabrics that don't wrinkle very much, such as synthetics and synthetic blends. More delicate items like wools, silks, and silk blends should always be air dried. Another trick to cut down on dryer time is to put things like towels in the dryer just long enough to fluff them up a bit, then hang them up to continue drying. Using indoor racks or clotheslines also humidifies your indoor air, which may come in handy in the winter. Bonus!

Getting the Greenest Machines

The washer wish list

Front-loading washing machines are the most eco-friendly, and thankfully, they're becoming easier to find in the average appliance store. They may cost more than top-loading washing machines, but in the long run they will be less expensive in terms of energy use costs and water savings: Front-loading machines may use as

much as 38 percent less water and 58 percent less energy.

Still, don't go trading in your perfectly good top-loader just to get a front-loader—that would be wasteful. When you are in the market for a new washer, you want to be sure to look for the most energy-efficient washing machine to meet your needs. Another priority is that your new washer should carry the Energy Star certification, which means it has been held up to an international standard of energy efficiency. Do research on your upcoming purchase through *Consumer Reports* magazine or other consumer-based organizations. There are many online resources that can help you determine what size and type of washer is best for you, including the Energy Star database at www.energystar.gov.

CLEANING CONUNDRUM

GAS OR ELECTRIC?

If you are in the market for a new washer or dryer, you may have a choice of whether to get electric or gas-operated machines. Gas installations may cost more to begin with, but they will turn out to be cheaper in the long run. For instance, according to the California Energy Center's Web site, it may cost 30 to 40 cents for each load of clothes you dry electrically, compared to 15 to 20 cents if your machine runs on gas.

The deal with dryers

While you should choose your washing machine very carefully when energy and water use are your prime considerations, the story is different for dryers. Despite the many brands and sizes on the market, they differ very little in terms of energy use. This is why you'll find that dryers do not carry the Energy Star label. A dryer typically ranks second, after refrigerators, in terms of the amount of energy you use in your home. As it stands, electric dryers are responsible for 5 to 10 percent of a home's electricity usage.

But there are still things you can do! For one, look for dryers with a moisture sensor setting, which can reduce the drying time. The sensor detects how much moisture is actually left in the clothes and will turn off the machine when moisture is gone, rather than waiting for a predetermined amount of time to pass. Most new models come with this feature, making your shopping job easier.

Developers are working on new machine-drying technologies, but not much has hit the market. Until a greener machine option is available, it's best if you use your dryer as little as possible, though when you do use it, do so efficiently.

The Fantastic Four in the Laundry Room

Now let's tackle green ways to clean those mucky clothes! Luckily, baking soda works as well in the laundry room as it does in the kitchen. Not only is it harmless to the environment, but it also has mild alkali qualities that help it dissolve grease and dirt. Baking soda can be especially helpful in areas served by hard water: Adding baking soda to a washing machine's rinse cycle will result in clothes that are better rinsed, and they will resist the stain buildup that can sometimes come with hard water. They'll also feel softer—another bonus!

When you use laundry detergent, add ½ cup baking soda to top-loading machines or ¼ cup for front-loading machines along with the usual amount of detergent to give the detergent a boost. The baking soda actually helps the detergent work better and acts as a deodorizer for some of those rougher-smelling clothes—like a teenager's sports gear and socks.

If you want to use bleach on some of your clothing, baking soda will help boost the bleach's whitening power so much that you'll be able to use less bleach—a good and green thing, indeed.

Salt, vinegar, and lemon juice also have roles to play in the laundry room. For starters, a basic mixture of half water and half vinegar makes a good pretreatment for just about any common stain. We suggest that you keep a spray bottle of this mixture in your laundry room. Just spray it onto the stain a few minutes before washing and then wash as usual.

Salt can also be a good stain remover in clothing, especially when the stain is still fresh. Salt's magic qualities also help maintain and restore bright colors, reduce yellowing, and eliminate mildew in fabrics. We'll get into the detailed instructions for these tricks a little bit later.

HEADS UP!

Do not apply any of the tips suggested here to clothes labeled "Dry Clean Only."

Like baking soda, vinegar can serve a lot of different purposes in the laundry room. When using vinegar in the laundry, use distilled white vinegar, which generally can be found in gallon jugs near the baking or laundry aisles in the grocery store. Apple cider vinegar will also work, but it usually comes in smaller containers and costs a little more.

Vinegar makes a great pretreatment for many stains, and it softens the water, helping to prevent soapy residue in homes that are served by hard water. It can also add a kick to both regular laundry detergents and some of the green commercial cleaners. To soften a standard load of wash, add ½ cup vinegar during your machine's last rinse cycle. In addition to softening, vinegar added at this time will help reduce lint buildup, and it tends to keep pesky pet hair from sticking to fabrics.

But among the Fantastic Four, lemon juice really takes the leading role for some laundry tasks. Add ½ cup of it to a regular load of laundry during the wash cycle, and it will make the whole load smell fresher. Add it to a load of whites, and the whites become whiter. Combine lemon juice with cream of tartar and you have a very powerful stain remover. We'll get into all that in more detail in a minute.

Eco-facts

According to *The Wall Street Journal,* Americans use 100 billion plastic shopping bags annually.

The Case Against Dry Cleaning

Frankly, dry cleaning isn't very eco-friendly, so why do we have to dry clean certain items in the first place? Generally, dry cleaning is required when there's a chance that water, soap, or detergent could damage the clothing's fabric. The key ingredient used in commercial dry cleaning is a chemical called tetrachloroethylene or perchloroethylene (PCE), which is generally referred to as dry cleaning fluid. This chemical is classified as a hazardous air contaminant by the Environmental Protection Agency (EPA) and is handled as a hazardous waste.

Unfortunately, it hasn't always been handled well in the United States; untold gallons have leached or have been dumped into supplies of drinking water. In fact, accidental or intentional dumping of PCEs into groundwater reservoirs happens so often that many commercial landlords will no longer lease space to dry cleaning operations.

Some new, greener dry cleaning methods are currently being developed, but at the time of publication, they are not widely used and are difficult to come by.

Dry cleaning solutions

So how do we get around the dry cleaning problem? Well, the first suggestion is an easy and obvious one: When shopping, don't buy items that require dry cleaning. Avoiding high-maintenance clothing has the added benefit of saving you money on dry cleaning bills.

DRYER BALL BOTHER

Currently, there's a trend toward buying "dryer balls," which claim to work like fabric softeners (by making your clothes soft and reducing static cling) and dry your clothes in less time. Made out of hard plastic with spiky things all over them, these balls look a bit like dog chew toys. The jury is definitely still out on whether the balls actually work as intended. A February 2008 study by *Consumer Reports,* however, reported that dryer balls did not stack up against liquid fabric softeners in either drying time or clothes softness.

However, perhaps there's a must-have item that's labeled as "dry clean only." Keep in mind that not all clothing tagged as such needs to be dry cleaned. In some cases, you may be able to clean the item at home. Some fabrics can be cleaned using a solution of 4 tablespoons baking soda in cold water. First, test a small, hidden area of the fabric to make sure it can handle the water and to see how colorfast it is. Also consider the importance of the item: You might not wish to try the baking soda method on your great-grandmother's brittle wedding dress. Sure, it might work, but just in case, it's best if you seek a professional opinion on how to clean a family heirloom.

Are Softeners Right for You?

You probably won't find any warning labels on a bottle of liquid fabric softener or a box of dryer sheets, yet these products may contain ingredients that can irritate skin and cause other health problems. While fabric softeners often contain fragrances and dyes that irritate the skin after getting into fabric, generally their ingredients are not hazardous to the environment. There's really no need to use a commercial softener, however. Its purpose is to bust static cling, and it does this by coating your clothing with a sort of waxy film.

If eliminating static cling is your aim, you can accomplish this on your own by using ¼ to ½ cup vinegar in your wash water. You can add the vinegar directly into the liquid softener cup, if your machine has one, or add it on top of the clothing during the rinse cycle. Our green goal, however, is to use less—ask yourself how many of your laundered items really *need* to have a softener added at all. For many items, adding softener is just an unnecessary luxury; you could eliminate a product or two, including vinegar, by washing those clothes or fabrics without softeners.

Fabric softener can build up on clothes over time, which ultimately reduces clothes' longevity. Parents should be aware that the accumulation can reduce the inflammability protectants in children's clothing. Just to be on the safe side, you should read the labels on your children's clothing and heed

the manufacturer's advice on whether or not to use fabric softener. It should also be noted that flame-retardant clothing for children does contain harmful PBDEs (polybrominated diphenyl ethers), which are known to cause thyroid problems in lab rats and are also linked to neurological damage.

To Bleach or Not to Bleach

You'll note that bleach is one of the items on our Terrible Ten list. Of course, bleach and bleachlike ingredients show up quite often in commercially available laundry detergents. It's also still quite common for people to use pure bleach when washing articles of clothing that need to get that elusive "whiter than white."

However, returning to our Fantastic Four list, there's an obvious bleach alternative: lemon juice. Straight lemon juice—either squeezed directly from the lemon or poured from a bottle—works very well for bleaching. Just about any fabric (except silk) can be bleached a whiter and brighter color by soaking it in a mixture of lemon juice and very hot water. First, mix ½ cup lemon juice with 1 gallon very hot water. Soak the clothing in it for at least one hour, though it can soak as long as overnight. Afterward, pour the lemon juice mixture into the washing machine, then wash the garment as usual.

Green Cleaning Stain Guide: Fabrics

Ink

Ink stains are some of the most
common types of stains we
get on our clothing—and are
among the most stubborn to
remove. Like a lot of the stains
mentioned here, ink can be
tackled with three of our Fan-

tastic Four items: salt, baking soda, and lemon juice.

Back in the day, we used to spray aerosol hair spray on
our clothes to make ink stains dissolve. It was certainly a smelly
option and probably not the best for our clothes (or, considering the fumes coming from the aerosol cans, ourselves). But
there certainly are other home remedies to try. For one, sprinkle a fresh stain with salt and then soak the entire garment in
milk; afterward, launder as usual.

Another method involves making a paste of lemon juice
and cream of tartar. You should first test the fabric for colorfastness: Paint the mixture onto a hidden area of the fabric and
let it sit for 20 minutes. If the color is fine, then it's full steam

ahead! Cover the stain with the paste and again let it sit for 20 minutes. Then check that the stain is removed before laundering the item as usual. An alternative method would be to cover the stain with cream of tartar and drizzle a little lemon juice onto it. Rub the mixture in and let it sit for a minute or two, then brush off any excess cream of tartar. Launder the item as usual.

Here's a tip for removing ink from white fabric: Apply the cream of tartar and lemon juice paste and then lay the fabric flat outside in a sunny spot. The paste will remove the stain, and the sun will brighten the white fabric. Then, of course, wash as usual.

Say you're at a party, and you've managed to swipe your pen on your shirt. Since most people don't carry cream of tartar and lemon juice everywhere they go, here's a trick to use in a pinch: Plain club soda helps keep stains from setting. Dip the

Eco-facts

In 2003, washing machines were 88 percent more energy efficient than they were in 1981.

stained area into the club soda and then dab with a hand-kerchief or other lint-free cloth. If the stain is serious, follow the methods mentioned already, or just launder as normal.

Red wine

Red wine can be removed from fabrics in some of the same ways as ink stains. Or, try this: Soak the stained  area in water, then make a pouch in the cloth where the wine stain is. Next, pour cream of tartar into the pouched area. Tie the ends of the pouch and then let the garment soak. After soaking, dip it in and out of hot water, then launder as usual.

Say it's a dinner party, and somebody got a little exuberant in conversation. If the red wine stain is fresh, soak up the spill by immediately sprinkling it with baking soda. Next, as soon as possible, stretch the stained fabric over a large bowl or kettle, secure the fabric, and pour boiling water through the stain. Similarly, you can use salt for this purpose by sprinkling it on a spill immediately and letting it soak up the stain. Afterward, soak the stained area in cold water and then launder the garment as usual.

> ### Eco-facts
> Currently, the United States recycles approximately 32 percent of its waste.

Blood

Bloodstains on cotton, linen, or other natural fiber fabrics should be soaked in cold salt water for one hour, then washed using warm water and your usual laundry soap. If you have a fresh bloodstain, cover it with salt and blot it with cold water. Add fresh water and blot until the stain is gone.

Candle wax

Handle with cold, then heat. First, place an ice cube on the wax. When the wax is hardened, remove it with a dull knife. Next, get rid of any remaining wax by putting a piece of thick paper (such as a paper bag) flat over the stain. Then press the area with a warm iron; the wax will melt into the paper.

Rust

Rust stains give us another laundry situation where cream of tartar is a great green hero—it has an acidic quality that enables it to break down rust. First, cover the rust stain with

THE DYNAMIC DUO VS. STUBBORN STAINS

If you've got a very stubborn stain, try this method: Mix equal parts white vinegar and lemon juice in a laundry tub or dishpan. Drop the stained garment in and let it soak for 30 minutes to an hour. Check the stain and launder as usual. After washing, check the stain again. If any stain remains, repeat the process above. Do not put the item into the dryer until the fabric is clean, as the heat will set the stain.

cream of tartar. Next, tie up the area surrounding the stain, making the fabric into a pouch. Soak the entire pouch in very hot water for about five to ten minutes, then untie it and launder as usual.

Salt and vinegar also work well as rust removers on fabric. Combine salt and vinegar into a thin paste and then spread the paste onto the stained area of the fabric. Next, lay the item out in the sun to bleach it. If sun is not an option, stretch the fabric over a large bowl or pan, secure the fabric, and pour boiling water through the stained area. Whether you use sun bleaching or the hot water method, allow the item to dry on its own. Run the item through a rinse cycle in your washing machine, or give it a good hand rinsing, and then check the stain again. If any of the stain remains, repeat the treatments. Never put the fabric through the dryer until you're certain the stain is gone.

Mildew

Make a thin paste of lemon juice and salt; spread the paste on mildew stains. Lay out the fabric in the sun to bleach it. Afterward, rinse and dry. Mildew stains on fabric can also be tackled with a paste of salt, vinegar, and water. If the stain is extensive, you can use up to full-strength vinegar.

Some garments may still retain a musty, mildewy smell even after washing. Get rid of the smell by soaking the garments in lemon juice and water and then letting them dry in the sun.

Gravy and grease

Dropping a bit of greasy gravy on your clothes can be a disaster, but not if you act quickly. Immediately after it happens, cover the fresh gravy stain with salt, letting it absorb as much of the grease as possible. Gently brush off the salt. If the stain is still visible, dab it with a cloth dipped in straight vinegar. This method can work for any fresh greasy spot.

GREEN CONFESSIONS: IRONING OUT THE ROUGH SPOTS

I gave up ironing in 1987. Life was just too short—why spend it ironing clothes? The fads in women's clothing during the early 1980s meant that women showed up at the office in mid-calf length natural cotton or linen skirts that required about a half hour of ironing each morning. Still, car commutes or the bus rides to work took their toll; by the time women arrived in the office, their carefully ironed clothing looked like it had been put through a wringer. I made the decision to buy fabrics that did not require ironing at all, or ones that would come unwrinkled enough simply by being tumbled in the dryer and then hung up immediately.

But the plan isn't always perfect—especially on those occasions when the clothes are left in the dryer, forgotten and wrinkled, for days. When this happens, a moral and environmental dilemma presents itself:

A. I could dampen and redry the clothes to avoid having to iron (bad green decision),

B. Iron them (heaven forbid!), or

C. Just wear them wrinkled.

Having to redry clothes wastes energy, but just as we mentioned at the beginning of this book, living a green life is a decision that takes effort. Just do what you can!

Coffee and tea

If you have an article of clothing
with set-in coffee or tea stains, don't
despair. Just soak it in a solution of
1 unit vinegar to 2 units water and
then hang the item to dry in the sun.
Still, the best treatment for coffee or

tea stains is to get them when they're fresh. When you tackle
the problem right away, the stains usually rinse out easily with
some cold water (depending upon the fabric).

Grass

As anyone who likes to spend time outdoors or
has rambunctious children can tell you, try-
ing to remove grass stains from white clothing
with the usual laundering techniques can be a
challenge. Try soaking the stained item in full-
strength vinegar for a half hour or more before
washing, then wash as usual.

Urine

First, soak the clothing in a solution of hot water and distilled
white vinegar. If the fabric is delicate, change the water

TOOL TIP **KEEPING YOUR IRON CLEAN**

Over time, you've probably had occasion to notice buildup or sticky spots on your iron's metal face. You can clean it off by running the iron at a very low setting over a piece of paper on which you've sprinkled some salt.

temperature to cold instead. Let it sit for a half hour, then rinse and wash as usual.

Juice

Reddish fruit juices of any kind—cherry, cranberry, blueberry— can be removed from bleach-safe garments by soaking them in a solution of 1 unit vinegar and 2 units water. Afterward, launder as usual.

Special Fabrics and Certain Situations

Yellowing

As fabric ages, it yellows—it's just a matter of fact. Older nylon fabrics, for example, yellow quite easily over time. You can help prevent yellowing in your favorite items by adding baking soda to both the wash and rinse cycles when laundering nylon items.

White linen items, such as fancy tablecloths, are also prone to yellowing. If yours have yellowed while in storage, brighten them up before your next dinner party by adding 4 tablespoons baking soda to the wash water. You can also boil yellowed cotton or linen fabrics in a mixture of water, 1 tablespoon salt, and ¼ cup baking soda. Bring to a boil and soak for an hour. Then launder as usual.

If you have linen, wool, or silk items that need to be hand washed, prevent them from yellowing by adding ½ cup vinegar to the rinse water.

Gum

It's easy to get that big wad of gum off an article of clothing, but the hard part is getting rid of the sticky residue the gum leaves behind. That residue can survive many a washing and live on to attract more dirt to  the spot. To take care of this problem, soak the sticky spot in undiluted vinegar for 10 to 15 minutes before washing, then launder as usual.

Crayon and bleeding colors

Accidents happen. Your child leaves a crayon in a pocket and you fail to find it before throwing the clothes into the washing machine. If you have a load of laundry riddled with crayon streaks, don't despair. Rewash the load using the hottest water the fabric will allow, and add ½ to 1 full small box baking soda to the load. You can also pretreat a crayon mark by sprinkling baking soda onto a damp cloth and then rubbing it into the fabric. Afterward, just launder as usual.

But we can't always blame laundry accidents on kids—sometimes it's our own doing. If you've managed to mix some colored clothes in with a load of whites, don't fret! You may not have done permanent damage. Before putting anything in the dryer, soak the damp clothes in a solution of baking soda and warm water to which you've added ½ cup salt and ½ cup detergent. Choose an earth-friendly detergent if you like, then wash as usual.

Swimsuit longevity

Chlorine in swimming pools can really do a number on your bathing

suit. Soak your suit in a sink of water to which 1 tablespoon baking soda has been added to minimize the fabric damage beforehand.

Perspiration

Even with frequent washing, perspiration can build up in clothing under the arms and around the collar. This is especially true in homes served by hard water. The more minerals in the

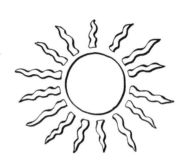

water, the harder it is to get stubborn residues out in the wash. Undissolved deodorants are often the culprits that contribute to the stains, so don't feel bad—your underarm stains may not be your fault!

To help remove perspiration stains on light-colored clothing, make a baking soda and water paste and paint it onto the stains with an old paintbrush. Let it sit for an hour or more, then launder as usual. If stains persist, apply the baking soda paste again, but try painting on a bit of undiluted vinegar first.

Leather shoes and other goods

Shoes and other leather items can also be cleaned with some of the Fantastic Four products. If you have dress shoes that need cleaning, try pouring a little lemon juice onto a soft cotton cloth and then sprinkling the cloth with cream of tartar. Use the cloth to massage the stained area lightly until the stain is removed. Lightly rinse the area and then buff it with another soft cloth. Light-colored shoes with black scuff marks can be shined with a baking soda paste. Rub the paste on with a soft cloth and then wipe it off. If you're going to apply a shoe polish, do it afterward.

If you happen to get ink on a leather item—say a ballpoint pen gets loose in your purse—baking soda can act as a mild scrubber. Just lay the item flat and sprinkle it with baking soda, lightly rubbing it in. Leave the baking soda on until the ink is absorbed, then brush it off. Repeat if necessary.

The white rubber soles on those expensive athletic shoes can also easily get scuffed up. You can clean off scuffs and black marks by sprinkling a little baking soda on a sponge or washcloth and wiping the stained areas.

Blankets

If you wash a cotton or other washable-fabric blanket in the washing machine, add 2 cups vinegar to the last rinse cycle. This will help to remove soap residue, and it will also make the blanket soft and fluffy.

Hand-washables

If you wash sweaters and delicate items by hand, add 1 or 2 tablespoons vinegar to the last rinse to help remove soap residue, which can be difficult to get out entirely when you hand wash. Silks, however, require a special hand washing treatment. Add 2 tablespoons vinegar to ½ cup mild detergent and mix with 2 quarts of cold water. Dip the silk item into the mixture, but *do not soak*. Rinse well and roll it in a heavy towel to soak up additional moisture. It's important to iron silks while they're still damp.

Laundering New Clothes

Some people are concerned about wearing newly purchased clothes before laundering them. This is because many new clothing items are treated at the factory with chemicals, including formaldehyde, that help them avoid mildew, resist wrinkling, or just look better for shipping and  purchasing. Some of these chemicals can cause skin irritation and possibly more serious ailments. To get the chemicals out of a fabric, first soak the item in a solution of ½ cup vinegar added to 1 gallon water. Rinse, then wash as directed by the garment's label.

Keeping new clothes looking, well, new

When washing a new item of clothing for the first time, add ½ cup salt to the wash cycle to prevent the colors from running. Salt can also help brighten up colored clothing that has become dull and dingy over time.

Colorfastness is often a problem with area rugs or curtains that have been hanging too long. If the curtain fabric is washable, add ½ cup salt to the wash cycle to help revamp the color. For nonwashable rugs, give them a brisk rub with a

---

GREEN NEWS: REUSING THE ALREADY RECYCLED

Ever wonder where all those old clothes you donate go? Nick Graham, founder of the underwear company Joe Boxer, has been doing something different with the donated clothes he finds. He has been gathering clothes from local Goodwill stores and has his designers reinvent them, using the preexisting clothing and fabrics to make new designs. Graham then sells them in trendy markets, splitting the profits with Goodwill Industries. More information (and many of the pieces) can be found at www.shopwilliamgood.com/Home.aspx.

cloth that has been dampened in salt water; allow them to dry thoroughly.

Another treatment for brightening up colored clothing is to soak the item in 1 gallon warm water and 1 cup vinegar. After soaking, rinse the item thoroughly with clear water.

Freshening Up

If you have loads of laundry stored in enclosed hampers or closets, just waiting to be done, sprinkle them with a little baking soda to control odors.
This is especially helpful if you have any young athletes in your house who are constantly producing sweaty clothing.

Odors that linger in your clothes even after laundering can be taken care of by adding baking soda to the rinse cycle. If you happen to have some clothes that smell like cigarette smoke, for example, try soaking them in a solution of baking soda and water first, then laundering as usual.

Sometimes hand-washables or table linens that have been stored away for a long time will need a little freshening up before they can be used. Help remove that stale storage smell by first soaking the item in a baking soda solution, then rinsing well and letting the item air dry.

A Guide to Greener Wear

Do fabrics matter?

Some people are so concerned about the environment that they have made the choice to buy and wear only all-natural and organic fiber clothing, including cotton, linen, wool, cashmere, silk, natural rayon (made from tree bark), and hemp. This is a great earth-conscious decision—though wearing nothing but natural fibers does doom these people to a lifetime of wrinkled clothing.

Convenience aside, many synthetic fabrics are derived from petroleum-based products, so it makes sense that we might want to limit our use of them. These include the following synthetic fibers:

- Acrylic
- Polyester
- Rayon
- Acetate
- Triacetate
- Nylon
- Clothing labeled *static-resistant, wrinkle-resistant, permanent press, no iron, stain-proof,* or *moth-repellent*

Special Delivery: Baby Laundry

Having a baby around the house gen-
erally means having mountains more
laundry to do—including your own,
which has been spit up on quite often. To
keep spit-up stains at bay, dab them as
soon as possible with a damp washcloth
that has been dipped in baking soda.
The odor will be controlled, and the stain won't set before you
have a chance to wash your clothes.

Even though many parents have not adopted eco-friendly
techniques for themselves, when it comes to baby's laundry,
they use only all-natural and nontoxic products. Well, with your
new green cleaning savvy, you now know that you can reach
for the baking soda to give your laundry soap or detergent of
choice an added boost. Just add ½ cup baking soda to your
soap or detergent for cleaner clothes that are good for the
earth and for your baby.

For new parents who are being showered with baby
clothes: First, enjoy it while it lasts! Next, remove any chemical
residues that the clothes may carry by washing everything with
mild soap and ½ cup baking soda. Rinse thoroughly.

KEEPING A GREEN HOUSE

Keeping your living space presentable and sanitary can sometimes feel like a daunting task—it seems as if there are always more clean-ing projects than time in the day! Day-to-day tidying is a must, not to mention those bigger clean-

ing projects (such as washing the windows or getting the dust out of the curtains) that must be tackled at least once a year.

But don't despair! Those same Fantastic Four cleaners we've been talking about all along—vinegar, salt, lemon juice, and baking soda—can make your household tasks less compli-cated and easier on you and the environment. We've already examined the best green cleaning techniques for the kitchen, bathroom, and laundry room, which are some of the most labor-intensive rooms in your home. While sometimes it may feel like you live in those rooms exclusively, let's now take a look around the rest of your home. It's time to grab your green cleaning kit from chapter 1 and get cracking!

Glass and mirrors

Forget ammonia-based window cleaners! The windows in your home can be effectively cleaned with 4 tablespoons lemon juice mixed with a half gallon of water. Other effective cleaners for glass and mirrors are rubbing alcohol and witch hazel.

TOOL TIP   MIRROR, MIRROR

Old-fashioned household hint books often say that you can wipe windows clean using newspapers. While this may sound like a totally green idea—after all, you'd be reusing newspapers and saving on paper towels—the reality is that doing so is messy and a big waste of time. Try using a clean, lint-free rag instead, perhaps an old cotton T-shirt or cloth diaper.

Vinyl

Dipping a cloth in straight lemon juice and rubbing it onto the stained area can remove stains on vinyl items such as recliners or tile flooring.

Furniture polishing

Furniture polish remains high on our list of the Terrible Ten because polish is usually made of petroleum distillates and solvents, both of which are hazardous and, well, smelly. At the very least, they're both poisonous, so why keep them around when there are plenty of earth-friendly ways to polish your wood items?

One very effective wood polish sounds like it would be a good salad dressing as well: Just mix 2 parts olive oil with 1 part lemon juice and apply it to your furniture using a soft cloth. The combination gives your wood furniture a nice smell and a sparkling shine.

When a hot serving dish or glass of water has marred the surface of a wood table, you can quickly get rid of the mark by making a thin paste of salad oil or lemon oil and salt. Wipe the paste on, then lightly buff the area as you wipe it off with a soft cloth.

> **Eco-facts**
>
> Approximately one-sixth of the wood used at a construction site gets tossed as waste and ends up in landfills.

Paint odors

Whenever you have an indoor painting project, you can help control the smell of the paint by keeping small dishes of vinegar scattered about in the room. The vinegar will absorb the paint odor while you work. Leave the dishes out for a few days after finishing the project to keep the paint smell at bay. Remember to change the vinegar each day.

Metal work

Metal polishes, such as those for brass, copper, stainless steel, and chrome, are also on our Terrible Ten list—and for good reason. Most metal polishes contain ammonia and usually at least one type of acid, among other undisclosed ingredients. This is another area where it's a good idea to try greener methods first before plunging into the use of harsh commercial products.

Do you have tarnished copper or brass antiques? Give them loads of shine without doing any damage by bringing in a couple of our Fantastic Four players—salt and vinegar—and adding one more ingredient from your kitchen cupboard: flour. Make a paste using equal parts of the three ingredients; rub the paste onto the brass or copper item with a soft cloth. Cover the entire surface and let the whole thing dry out (this will take about an hour). Wipe off the dried paste with a clean, soft cloth.

Lemon can also be used for lightly tarnished brass or copper pieces. Slice one lemon and dip it in salt, then rub the item with the salted lemon. Afterward, rinse and dry thoroughly.

Another fix for lightly tarnished copper is to use a spray bottle filled with undiluted vinegar. Just spray the copper piece and sprinkle the tarnished area with salt. Wipe thoroughly with a sponge or cotton cloth; be sure to remove all the salt, or the item will turn green. Repeat if necessary.

Fireplace

If your wood-burning fireplace has gathered soot and smoke smudges around its exterior, you can spruce it up by applying a paste of cream of tartar and water. Rub the paste into the stains, let it dry, then scrub it off.

Pewter Polishing

Because it is a soft metal and can be easily damaged, pewter must be given special care. To give your pewter items a refreshed glow, try this homemade, all-green cleaner:

Mix 1 teaspoon salt and 1 cup vinegar. Add enough flour to the mixture to make a paste. Apply the paste using a soft cloth and allow it to dry for half an hour. Rinse the piece thoroughly with warm water and polish with another soft cloth. Make sure all the paste is removed from any grooves or hidden areas.

If it's the inside of your fireplace and chimney you're worried about, you can help loosen soot buildup by tossing an occasional handful of salt into the fire the next time you're enjoying your fireplace. The burning salt will help loosen the soot a little, buying you some time between major cleanings.

Keeping Things Fresh

In the first chapter, we talked about the need to avoid aerosols, such as those found with a typical room air-freshening sprayer. You can achieve the same effect—a clean, fresh-smelling house—with your own nontoxic concoctions. As an added bonus, you can mix and match scents to suit your own fragrance tastes!

DIY freshener

The human sense of smell is a very sensitive thing, so much so that a clean-smelling home can play a large part in your emotional and physical health. Make your own earth-friendly freshener spray by mixing equal parts lemon juice and water and storing it in a spray bottle you've salvaged from some of your old cleaning products (make sure to rinse it out well first). Spray this around your home once or twice a week for odor control, or as needed when cooking or to get rid of smells that have seeped into the draperies, couch, and other fabrics.

Simmering scents

One way to spice up your home is by simmering a little cinnamon, cloves, fresh ginger, and the herbs of your choice in a bit of water on your stovetop. For a more summery smell, try adding a handful of mint leaves to 8 cups water. Bring the mixture to a boil first and then turn down to a simmer. You can also use essential oils in combination with these spices, or alone.

Scent on the spot

For rooms that need freshening in a jiff, soak cotton balls in vanilla extract or an essential oil. Place the cotton in a pretty dish or jar wherever you need to refresh the air. You can also just pour a little vanilla extract into a small bowl and place it where needed.

An essential oils tutorial

Since we're on the topic of smell, now is a perfect time to talk about essential oils. We've already mentioned a few: lavender,

Eco-facts

One tree releases enough oxygen into the air to support two human beings.

ylang-ylang, patchouli, clove, vanilla, and peppermint. Many of these may already be found in any ordinary garden or in your kitchen cabinets. You may have also seen them on the labels of many cleaning products, especially those that feature the buzzwords "all-natural," "hypoallergenic," and "organic." A word of caution, though: Just because something is natural, it isn't necessarily hypoallergenic. Some people are allergic to even all-natural products.

Essential oils are quite versatile. They are mostly plant-derived, with the exception of musk, which is taken from the musk glands of a large mammal—usually the musk ox. The plant-based essential oils are extracted from the leaves, stems, or stalks of the plant through a process of cold- or hot-pressing. For centuries, plants have been used for their different effects on the human body. As more and more people look for greener alternatives for their lifestyles, the many uses of essential oils—everything from aromatherapy to cleaning and pest control—have had a resurgence in popularity. Much like the Fantastic Four ingredients of green cleaning, there is the fabulous core group of essential oils: eucalyptus, lavender, peppermint, and citrus.

Essential oils can be suspended in another inert oil, such as mineral oil or another plant-based oil like carrot or apricot seed oil. They can also be combined in a solution with rubbing alcohol and witch hazel. They can't be used with water, since, as you might remember from high school chemistry class, oil and water do not mix. Essential oils can also be used with the Fantastic Four in various household tasks or added to lotions and salves—just don't apply them directly to laundry or they'll stain. In some cases (though not for people who are allergic, are in early pregnancy, or are nursing), oils are safe to inhale or ingest. Of course, make sure to research the safety of an oil first and use where appropriate.

Now, let's take a closer look at these four oils:

Eucalyptus oil has antibacterial and disinfecting powers—a few drops added to your mop water can make your floors smell and look better. Eucalyptus oil also works well as an effective insect repellent. However, it does yield a stronger scent than, say, lavender oil. When using it as an air freshener, first dilute it with water.

Lavender oil is often used in homemade sprays and sachets. It not only freshens rooms and closets, it keeps away

mosquitoes, flies, gnats, and other biting insects. It is also bothersome to moths; when combined with cedar chips or slivers, lavender oil makes a powerful moth repellent. Sprays or lotions made with lavender oil can be used directly on the skin as chemical-free insect repellent. However, be sure to reapply often; depending on the suspension medium (alcohol versus lotion), it may evaporate faster than typical commercial bug repellents. Lavender oil in soy candles, placed around the home or garden, has a bug-repelling effect that is more powerful than citronella—and it smells nicer, too. For maximum effect, combine lavender oil with eucalyptus and clove oils. Lavender is also a highly effective disinfectant with antibacterial properties and can be used in garbage and diaper pails. It can be used in a solution to refresh and disinfect nonporous surfaces like countertops and porous surfaces like draperies, upholstery, and bedding.

Peppermint oil smells nice and fresh, but it also can be used to stave away vermin such as ants, roaches, and mice. Using the oil in its undiluted form and placing it in your home at entrances and around the perimeters of a room (particularly a room that has an exterior wall) will keep the vermin from crossing into your home. Like the other oils, a few drops of peppermint oil can be placed in a pot of water set to simmer to help quickly rid the home of bothersome odors.

Citrus oils such as lemon, lime, and grapefruit oils, as well as our fantastic friend lemon juice, can be used in a variety of applications, even as polish for wood floors and wood furniture. Depending upon how severely dry the wood is, citrus oils can be either applied directly or suspended in another inert oil medium. Do not use citrus oils on cooking utensils, however. Citrus oils are also good for removing stickers and other gooey items—just add a couple of drops of the oil to the sticker and rub with a damp cloth until the adhesive is gone.

Houseplants: a natural cleaning tool

NASA (the National Aeronautics and Space Administration) has determined that some common houseplants can do a world of good at eliminating nasty toxins that may be in your home. After all, indoor air quality is a matter of some concern: Along with everyday carcinogens such as secondhand smoke (which contains sulfur dioxide), common household products may also be emitting chemicals into the air we breathe. One of these chemicals is formaldehyde, which can be found in clothes, plywood, and carpeting, leading to headaches and breathing problems.

NASA studied three common indoor pollutants—trichloroethylene, formaldehyde, and benzene—and concluded that the average home could benefit from keeping about 15 plants around. Plants work to gently remove these toxins from your indoor air by producing oxygen, adding moisture to the air, and absorbing the bad stuff through their leaves. Consider them nature's filter!

Here are some houseplants to consider adding to your indoor plant collection:

The Boston fern (Nephrolepi exalta "Bostoniensis"), florist's mum (Chrysanthemum morifolium), gerbera daisy (Gerbera jamesonii), dwarf date palm (Phoenix roebelenii), areca palm

(*Chrysalidocarpus lutescens*), moth orchid (*Phalenopsis*), bamboo palm (*Chamaedorea*), Chinese evergreen (*Aglaonema*), English ivy (*Hedera helix*), indoor dracaenas (*Dracaena* "Janet Craig," *D. marginata*, *D. massangeana*, and *D. warnekii*), and the snake plant or mother-in-law's tongue (*Sansevieria trifasciata laurentii*).

Reduce Your Space: Moving into a Smaller Home

It may sound overly simplistic, but one way to save time and energy on cleaning—not to mention energy resources—is to live in a smaller home. Too many of us are occupying more space than we really need. Over the past three decades, house sizes in the United States have been steadily growing. In 1970, new

homes built in the United States averaged 1,500 square feet. In 2001, the average was more than 2,300 square feet, even though fewer people are living in each home (smaller families are the norm now, compared to the '70s).

If you're in the market for a new home, carefully consider how much space you really need. Most of us spend the bulk of our time in very few of our home's total rooms. Often we'll dedicate a room to one specific purpose (the sewing room, the guest room) only to have it sit idle, gathering dust for months on end. To make the most of your space, think "multiple use" when choosing or designing a home based on the number of rooms.

Several nonprofit organizations and trade groups dedicated to building smaller houses have sprung up to address the trend toward ever larger homes in the United States. In fact, they're being successful in some areas—Los Angeles, California; Edina, Minnesota; Wellesley, Massachusetts; Atlanta, Georgia; and Austin, Texas, are among the cities that have recently considered setting an upper limit on house size in certain parts of their city, based on the theory that large houses are a huge drain on community resources. Developers have cried foul over these efforts—every American has a right to own a Mega Mansion, after all—but a case can be made about the drain on publicly controlled natural resources when homes are too large. If this sort of downsizing is of interest to you, here are some organizations to look into:

- Resources for Life, www.resourcesforlife.com
- Tumbleweed Tiny House Company, www.tumbleweedhouses.com
- Little House on a Small Planet, www.littlehouseonasmallplanet.com

Passing the Clutter Around

Cleaning your home can also lead to a massive decluttering of your house. Often after a big cleaning binge, you may find that you've accumulated a small mountain of items that you don't need anymore. If any of it is reusable,  you may want to consider joining an online community called Freecycle (www.freecycle.org), which has localized chapters of members who let each other know what stuff they have hanging around that they would like to give away—anything from kitchen appliances, bicycles, and furniture to magazines, clothing, and diapers (unused, of course!).

The Freecycle community takes place entirely online, after you sign up to be a part of an e-mail group (also called a list-serv). The groups are local even though Freecycle is a

Eco-facts

By recycling one glass bottle, enough energy is saved to light a standard lightbulb for four hours.

nation-wide program. It's a great way to declutter the house and provide somebody else with something they need—all without the hassle of staging your own yard sale. Plus, moving around possessions already in existence is a way to prevent more goods from being manufactured or being dumped into a landfill.

Similarly, you might look into turning other outdated items over to charitable programs such as the DAV (Disabled American Veterans), Goodwill, or the Salvation Army. There are also organizations that will take your old electronics (such as computers and cell phones), your printer cartridges, your eyeglasses, and even your sneakers and distribute them to others who need them. A simple Internet search will offer many options to help you get rid of some of these items in your home. Check page 157 for a list of more resources to consider.

Greening Up the Inner Workings

You diligently clean your house daily or weekly as needed, perhaps also doing big cleaning projects twice a year. This is all well and good, but do you give your home's infrastructure a regular cleaning? Your heating and cooling air ducts should also be inspected and cleaned on a regular basis. If you've been in your home for a while and have never had your air ducts inspected, it may be time to do so. After all, the air that flows around your home affects your health as much as dirt and grime buildup!

The federal Environmental Protection Agency (EPA) recommends that a professional heating and cooling contractor inspect your home's air ducts and heating and cooling systems. If the contractor sees signs of mold, dust, dirt, and other contaminants, or if he or she notices a musty odor in the ductwork, having your ducts and systems cleaned will be recommended. If that's the case, you should consider hiring a professional duct cleaner—this is probably not a job you can safely do on your own.

Magic Carpet Cleaners

The first rule of green carpet cleaning is to clean up any spill or stain immediately. By doing so, you'll avoid more heavy-duty cleaning down the road.

Beyond that, it's advisable to check the manufacturer's label for care instructions before attempting to clean a rug or carpet on your own. Still, you should generally be safe using our Fantastic Four ingredients. For everyday cleanup, use equal parts vinegar and water, lightly sponging the mixture into the carpet. Rinse the area and blot dry, then let it air dry completely.

Should there be a smudge or spill on your rug or carpet, sprinkle it with baking soda, salt, or cornstarch and allow it

TOOL TIP CREATE-YOUR-OWN CARPET CLEANER

With a little whisking, you can have your own safe and natural foaming rug cleaner ready to go! Mix 1/4 cup mild liquid laundry detergent with 1 cup water. Beat the mixture with an egg-beater, or whisk it until it froths up like the foam on a latte. Using a sponge or cotton cloth, wipe a small amount of the mixture onto the rug and rub it in gently. Repeat as needed; afterward, wipe the sponged area dry with a clean rag.

to sit for a while. Afterward, vacuum to remove the cleaning product from the carpet.

After the big clean

If you use a carpet-cleaning machine to give your rugs and carpets heavy-duty cleaning, take the next step and give your carpet this special green rinsing treatment afterward. It will help your carpet stay fresh and clean longer, because you'll be removing any excess shampoo residue (helping you avoid more frequent shampoos and saving you time and energy). After a normal machine cleaning, combine ¼ cup vinegar with 1 gallon water; add this to your machine and run it as you normally would.

TOOL TIP **DIG THE DIAPER**

Absorbent, strong, and lint-free, plain cloth diapers are excellent for most household cleaning tasks, including cleaning up floors, furniture, and mirrors. If you use cloth diapers for your infant, reuse the outgrown sizes by repurposing them for every-day cleaning. This is especially useful if you don't plan to save the diapers for another baby. And, unlike paper towels, instead of tossing them in the trash, you can just toss them in the laundry. For those who aren't already familiar with the wonders of cloth diapers, you can buy large packages of them in the baby aisle of almost any major general merchandise store.

Green Cleaning Stain Guide: Carpets

Commercial spot removers for carpets and rugs usually contain caustic substances, not to mention chlorine and/or petroleum-based solvents. Although more and more spot removers are becoming available that claim to be easy on both the environ-

Standby Carpet Freshener

Company coming over? You can make your own nontoxic everyday carpet freshener to use as needed. Choose 1 cup of crushed, dried herbs of your choice—rosemary, lavender, and southernwood are all good choices to get you started. Add 1 teaspoon ground cloves, 1 teaspoon cinnamon, and 2 teaspoons baking soda. Combine all of these and store in a lidded container. Shake it well before using and then sprinkle the mixture on your carpet. Let it sit for 15 minutes, then vacuum up. Doing this will make the room smell nice and will neutralize carpet odors.

ment and your health, there's really no need for you to buy them. Luckily, you can tackle many of the common carpet and rug stains you may encounter with a vinegar and water solution, and sometimes with just undiluted vinegar alone! To get that coveted foaming action that many products feature, place the vinegar solution into a well-rinsed foaming soap bottle.

Now, let's look at some specific situations where green cleaning can be applied to the carpet.

Crayons and glue

With kids in the house, you might find chewing gum or crayon stains mysteriously appearing in your rug or carpet (try finding a kid to

own up to them!). For each of these, you need to use undiluted vinegar. To remove crayon stains, tackle the spot directly by dipping an old toothbrush in vinegar and scrubbing the stained area.

If you find a dried blob of white school glue on your carpet, try treating it with a vinegar and water solution sponged in and blotted. However, if the spot is stubborn, warm up the vinegar a little bit on the stove or in your microwave and sponge it in undiluted. Let it sit for 10 to 15 minutes, then scrape it away. Clean up any residue using the vinegar and water solution.

Greasy spills

Here's an excellent way to pick up a greasy spill on your carpet: Sprinkle it with a little cornmeal and allow it to sit for five minutes. Next, sponge the area with vinegar and water.

The Four Cs: Catsup, Chocolate, Coffee, and Cola

When your rug or carpet is stained with any one of the Four Cs, a vinegar and water solution is called for. Remember, though, that each culprit requires an individual application guideline. For each, first mix 1 cup vinegar with 2 cups water (or a 1:2 ratio of any kind, depending upon the quantity you need).

For catsup, liberally sponge the mixture into the carpet until the stain disappears, rinsing and repeatedly wringing out your sponge.

Chocolate stains should be treated in the same way, but it's important to blot with a clean cloth, rather than rub, to avoid spreading the stain further. Again, rinse and wring out your sponge repeatedly until the water runs clear.

A coffee or tea spill on the rug should come up easily if you catch it right away. Just sponge it with clean water. If the stain is set, however, use the vinegar and water solution; sponge it in, then rinse and wring until all brown color is gone. You can treat dark cola stains in the same way.

Mildew

It's certainly not unusual for a rug or carpet to suffer some kind of accidental saturation—from a leaky roof, an overfilled bathtub, an actual flood, or perhaps simply a spilled glass of juice. Whatever the liquid, your only defense is to get it dried out as quickly as possible. Still, it's probably safe to assume you're going to have a mildew problem anyway; after all, mildew loves the damp, and rugs love to retain dampness.

You can kill any mildew hiding in your rug fibers by sponging in a mixture of half vinegar and half water. But you must take measures to ensure the rug dries thoroughly. If you can't set the rug or carpet out in the sun for a long time, you may want to use a hair dryer, set at a very low setting, and/or aim some electric fans at it. The goal, after all, is to defeat dampness!

Red wine

When you have a brand-new red wine

spill on a light-colored

carpet, sprinkle the spill

with salt and let it sit for 15 minutes. The salt will absorb the

spill and will turn pink. After brushing or vacuuming the salt

away, clean the area with a mixture of ⅓ cup vinegar and

⅔ cup water.

Cleaning Bare Floors

Your basic vinegar and water solution is really the perfect
choice for cleaning most types of bare floors in your home.
Mix up 1 cup vinegar with 1 gallon warm water (be sure
it's warm!) and mop it onto a ceramic tile, linoleum, vinyl,
or wood floor. There is no need to rinse afterward—saving
both time and water. If your vinyl or linoleum floor looks a
little dull after cleaning, you can give it a shine by mopping it
over again with straight club soda. Try not to saturate wood
floors with the vinegar and water solution. Use a light touch;
the mixture will make your floor shiny and remove any greasy
buildup.

Babies: Bundles of Joy, Lots of Messes

Babies sure take up a lot of time. There's the feeding, the clothing, the rocking, the consoling. They're also incredibly messy. Still, you probably wouldn't dream of bringing harsh cleaners into your baby's nursery, or cleaning the assorted toys, pacifiers, and hygiene products with them. Our green cleaning kit (starring the Fantastic Four) is great for keeping most of baby's things clean, sanitary, and smelling fresh.

Again, baking soda is the star of the show when it comes to the general cleaning of your children's belongings. Safely clean the crib and baby mattress by wiping them down with a damp sponge sprinkled with baking soda. Changing tables and playpens are more great places to use baking soda. Be sure to rinse thoroughly!

For green cleanups on the go, mix up a baking soda and water solution in a small, closeable spray

bottle. Take this bottle with you on outings and you'll be ready for nearly anything.

Baking soda on a damp sponge is also a great way to clean any metal, plastic, or vinyl surface on strollers, car seats, and high chairs. Just be sure to wipe and rinse thoroughly.

Toy care

Baby toys can get grungy and smelly in no time flat. Clean noncloth toys in the same way you would the crib and mattress, with a damp sponge or cloth sprinkled with baking soda, making sure to rinse and dry thoroughly. For cloth toys, just sprinkle them thoroughly with baking soda and let sit for 15 minutes. Then brush or vacuum off the baking soda with a handheld vacuum.

TOOL TIP   TOY CLEANING TIME-SAVER

It can be a real pain to hand clean each of your child's toys. Cut down the time spent cleaning by herding a bunch of small stuffed animals into a large plastic garbage bag and sprinkling in a generous amount of baking soda. Close the bag up so nothing flies out and give it a good shake, getting all the animals covered in baking soda. Let the bag sit for an hour and then remove. Dust off each animal—now your child's favorite friends are ready to go!

Odor patrol

You can eliminate lingering odors in cloth strollers or car seats by sprinkling them with baking soda. Wait 15 minutes and then vacuum thoroughly.

It probably goes without saying that you can keep a diaper pail smelling fresh if you cover the bottom with baking soda. Sprinkle a little baking soda on top each time you add a new diaper to the pail.

Rugs

You can clean and deodorize any of baby's accidents on your rug or carpet by first soaking up as much of it as possible using a sponge or rag. Afterward, sprinkle the area with baking soda and let it dry. Vacuum after drying.

Combs and brushes

Give baby's personal hygiene tools—including baby combs and brushes—a good cleaning by filling your bathroom sink with water and adding 1 teaspoon baking soda. Swish the combs and brushes around in the water, rinse well, and dry.

Baby bottles

Clean and deodorize baby bottles by filling them with warm water and adding 1 teaspoon baking soda. Close and shake vigorously, then rinse and clean as usual.

Bottle nipples and bottle brushes can be freshened up overnight by soaking them in a mixture of 4 tablespoons baking soda per 1 quart hot water. Drain, rinse, and clean as normal in the morning.

The Pet Patrol

We've already shown that our Fantastic Four list of green cleaning ingredients is great in a variety of cleaning situations. But since these ingredients are nontoxic and safe to use around animals, they make special sense in households with pets.

Accidents and odors

If your pet has had an accident, scrub the area with club soda as soon as possible and let it dry. Then sprinkle the area with baking soda and let it stand to help control odors. After an hour or so, vacuum the rug thoroughly.

If a stain or discoloration remains, apply a generous amount of lemon juice to the area; let it soak for about 15 to 30 minutes. When the stain is removed, rinse the area well

> **TOOTHY TIP**
> Baking soda makes a great natural toothpaste for both humans and pets. For your dog or cat, dip a small, soft-bristled toothbrush into baking soda and brush gently.

and blot it thoroughly. Another remedy to try is a paste made with lemon juice and cream of tartar, followed by the same rinsing and blotting technique.

After the stain removal, deodorize if necessary by rinsing the area with a vinegar and water solution. It's important to remove the odor—doing so helps give your pet the signal that they should not do the same thing in that spot again.

If the accident was fairly small, say, a simple spot of urine on a rug, it can be cleaned up by applying straight vinegar to the area with a sponge or rag. Let it dry, then spend some time giving your pet a refresher course in potty training.

Bath time

Does Whiskers smell funky? Has Mr. Sprinkles gotten into something rank? Baking soda is a great option for dry bathing your pet. This is especially helpful since most cats hate water. To dry bathe your dog or cat, sprinkle your pet's coat with baking soda, then give the coat a good rubdown with your hands. Next, use a gentle brush to spread the baking soda throughout the coat until the baking soda is gone. And since it is nontoxic, there's no need to worry if your pet takes a liking to its taste.

If you want to minimize soap residue when using other dog-washing methods, add a little vinegar to the rinse water after the bath, then rinse your dog again with plain water.

Pet bedding

Perhaps your dog has a favorite pillow it snuggles up with. This is all well and good, but every now and then you might want to make it smell a little less doglike. You can do this by sprinkling the bedding with baking soda, letting it stand 15 minutes, then vacuuming thoroughly.

Cat litter

Clean the cat litter pan by removing the soiled litter and pouring in ½ inch vinegar. Let it stand for ten minutes or so, then pour out and dry. To control odors before filling again, sprinkle ½ cup baking soda over the bottom of the pan.

Some people have environmental and health concerns about the type of cat litter available commercially. Pregnant women especially are at risk for a virus called toxoplasmosis, which can be contracted by handling cat litter, the litter box,

---

KITTY TIP

To discourage your cats from walking on, sleeping on, or scratching certain items in your home, lightly sprinkle the area with vinegar. The smell will keep cats away!

---

or the box liner. Try to keep your cat's litter box area clean at all times to reduce the risk, but pregnant women should avoid handling anything to do with cat litter for the duration of their pregnancy.

If you're really ambitious, you can make your own natural cat litter. Just mix a small box of baking soda with two to three inches of dry, sandy clay soil.

The flea fight

You don't need to use a commercial flea shampoo to get rid of pesky fleas on your pet. The usual pet shampoos contain chemicals that we can all live without, and the truth is, soap and water will kill the fleas just fine—the trick is to leave the soap and water on your pet for five to eight minutes.

Birds, ferrets, and other caged critters

Most bird and rabbit cages, ferret houses, hamster homes, and the like can be adequately cleaned by wiping them down with a sponge sprinkled with baking soda or dampened with vinegar.

Both of these are especially good with urine smells and stains. You might also want to add a thin layer of baking soda on the floor of the cage after cleaning to help control odors.

Fishy fish tank

When it's time to clean out the fish tank, clean the inside of the glass with plain noniodized salt by sprinkling it onto a damp

sponge and scrubbing. This will remove hard water deposits or other buildup on the glass. Rinse everything well before returning the fish to the tank.

Aquarium redecoration

You certainly don't want to introduce strange organisms into your delicate aquarium, but you can still go out and collect some stones for the bottom—just be sure to clean the stones thoroughly before adding them into your fish habitat. Clean the stones by scrubbing them with undiluted vinegar. However, if your rock fizzes up when you apply the vinegar, discard the stone, as it probably will affect the pH balance of your tank.

CAR KEEPERS AND GARAGE SWEEPERS

Many people rarely wash their car, on the theory that it's just going to get dirty again and, eventually, it will rain and the car will get cleaned that way. However, a case can be made for regular car washing to keep salt (in northern climes) at bay and grit and grime off the finish. Road salt, dirt, and pollution can all lead to damaged paint jobs. Keeping your exterior clean helps prolong the finish on your car and can ultimately prevent corrosion that could threaten your car's overall life span. If you can keep corrosion at bay, you will probably keep your car longer—that's good both for you and for the planet.

Still, if you're thinking it's more earth-friendly to wash your car at home in your driveway, you're wrong. Studies have shown that a commercial car wash uses up to 60 percent less water than washing your car at home with, say, water from a garden hose. According to one study, a typical commercial car wash used 20 to 45 gallons of water. Compare that to the

GREENER WAYS TO WASH YOUR CAR

- Wash your car only when necessary.
- If you can, park your car on your lawn while you wash it. The lawn will act as a filter to keep soils, soap, and oil from traveling directly into storm drains.
- Use a hose nozzle that allows you to control the flow of water. Also, fill up buckets of water only as needed.
- Collect rainwater or some other slightly used water from your household to use for washing the car.
- Use the Fantastic Four ingredients whenever possible.

estimated 140 gallons of water used during a home car wash. Also, as an added bonus, most car washes recycle the water.

In this chapter, we'll take a look at some green ways to wash and maintain your car and garage.

The Race Is On!

You can use a baking soda solution of 1 cup baking soda to 1 gallon water to safely clean many parts of your car: Using a soft rag, clean the headlights and taillights, the chrome trim, windows, tires, vinyl seating, and floor mats.

Wipe the dashboard, steering wheel, and interior trim with a damp cloth or mild cleaner. Try using a cotton swab to reach small spaces such as coin holders.

Upholstery

If your car's cloth upholstery is stained, don't fret! Instead, make a baking soda paste and rub it into the stain. Allow it to dry, then vacuum up the residue.

Many people eat entire meals while riding in the car, so it's no wonder that vinyl seats can become easily stained with oil and grease. Remove these greasy stains by wiping them with a rag that has been dipped in a solution of baking soda and water. You can also try sprinkling baking soda directly

---

T_{OOL} **PET HAIR IN THE UPHOLSTERY**
TIP

If your dog is allowed to ride in the car, no doubt he or she leaves behind plenty of hair. Sometimes the fluff just won't come off your cloth upholstery even with a vacuum or powerful wet/dry vac—it's pretty stubborn stuff. When that happens, put on a pair of latex gloves. Run your gloved hands over the hairy areas of your car, and the hair usually will come off onto the glove. It's a static electricity thing, and it works pretty well!

---

onto the stain and wiping with a damp sponge. For both, rinse and wipe clean.

Odor control

Maybe it's your pets or maybe it's your proclivity toward eating slices of pizza while driving—either way, your car is taking on odors that even driving with the windows down doesn't eliminate. If your car is getting a little smelly, don't pull out the spray air freshener from your home or hang one of those overperfumed bits of cardboard from your rearview mirror. Instead, control odors by placing a jar filled with baking soda in one of your available cup holders. Punch holes in the lid of the jar—big enough to let the baking soda work its deodorizing magic, but not big enough to spill the contents. Change the baking soda in your jar once a month.

Oil spillage

Okay, it's not exactly the *Exxon Valdez,* but it's still a big mess when an oil spill mars your clean cement garage floor. If the spill is new, sprinkle it entirely with salt and wait 15 minutes. The salt acts as an absorbent and will do the trick quite nicely. No doubt a spot will remain, but this first treatment is a step toward helping you remove it entirely.

GENERAL CAR CLEANING TIPS

Here's a neat little list of green car-care tips provided by the Lake Whatcom Management Program in Bellingham, Washington, which cares about the water quality in its community:

- **To clean the car body:** Choose a phosphate-free and nontoxic soap; use as little as possible.
- **To scour:** Apply baking soda.
- **To clean fiberglass:** Use a baking soda paste.
- **To clean windows:** 1 cup vinegar with 1 cup warm water. Rinse and squeegee dry.
- **To clean aluminum:** 2 tablespoons cream of tartar in 1 quart hot water.
- **To clean and polish chrome:** Apply apple cider vinegar to clean; use baby oil to polish.

Now, for stain removal, mix equal parts baking soda and cornmeal and sprinkle the mixture onto the remaining spot. Let it dry, and then sweep or vacuum the mixture away. For tougher spots, or for stains that have been there a while, sprinkle baking soda onto the spot, let it stand 15 minutes, and then attack it with a wet, stiff-bristled brush.

If you're a handy person who changes your own oil, be sure to properly dispose of your old oil according to local ordinance. Just a single quart of motor oil can contaminate up to 250,000 gallons of fresh water if disposed of improperly!

Battery leaks

If you have the misfortune of having a car battery leak acid onto your garage floor, you'll want to contain it and clean it up as soon as possible. First, apply baking soda to the spill. To provide you with a benchmark as to how much baking soda you'll need, consider that 1 pound of baking soda will neutralize 1 pint of acid.

Winning at car windows

You may wonder how the inside of your car windows get so dirty when they're not exposed to the outside elements. It turns out the vinyl and plastics in the average car give off fumes and

---

RAINWATER RECON

We should all be mindful of how much water we use, but in some areas of the United States and Canada, water is in critically short supply to begin with, and things may get worse in the near future. At last count, the federal government projects that some 36 states will face water shortages in the coming years because of drought, potential population growth, urban sprawl, rising temperatures, and, you guessed it, excessive use.

For random house projects, you might consider saving water by collecting rainwater just like they used to do in the old days. Collect the rainwater drainage from your house's downspouts in a barrel or bucket and top with a lid to prevent evaporation. Then use the collected water for such tasks as washing the car, watering the lawn, or washing down the house windows and screens in the spring. Doing so will help you do your part toward conservation by having a little bit of your own water supply, which will prove especially helpful if your area is headed for a drought. For instance, if the roof on your house is 1,000 square feet, and you happen to have an average annual rainfall of 20 inches, you could potentially collect 24,000 gallons of water annually!

oils that create a filmy buildup on the inside of your windows. (On second thought, maybe you don't want to think about that!)

To clean them, you'll need to cut through the grime. You can do this by applying the same window-cleaning techniques we mentioned on page 105: Use 4 tablespoons lemon juice mixed with ½ gallon water. Wipe the cleaner onto the windows, both inside and out, and wipe dry with a cotton cloth.

Sign of the times

If your bumper is covered with stickers and you've since changed your mind about the candidates or bands you (or the car's previous owner) used to promote, you can remove these easily using one of two methods. First, warm the sticker with a hair dryer and then attempt to peel the sticker back. If any sticky residue remains, wipe it with a bit of vegetable oil to remove the stickiness. (General rule: Oily removes sticky.)

If you'd rather, try first saturating the sticker with vegetable oil and letting it sit for a while. Afterward, peel it back using the same method.

The Green Garage

We all know the garage is one of the many places in the home where old stuff goes to linger. Sure, it's easy to go out to the garage with every intent to clean the place up, but it's  equally easy to be daunted by the task. If you find old belongings lingering in your rafters or stuffed behind the tricycles your college-age kids don't seem to use anymore, try the green cleaning and decluttering tips that follow. The same rules apply here for getting rid of stuff as we mentioned in chapter 5: Yard sales, charity donations, and Freecycle are always options. If you're not using it, you probably don't need to keep it. Repurpose what you can, then give the rest away.

> **Eco-facts**
> Do the math: Most Americans toss out an average of about four pounds of garbage every day!

The musty...

Canvas items such as old-fashioned tents, old army cots, and long-neglected athletic bags are likely to have developed a rather musty smell when you finally uncover them. If you plan to keep these items, give them a special treatment to remove that smell.

If it's a bag with a zipper, sprinkle a generous amount of baking soda or salt into the bag and close it up overnight. The next day, dump out the salt or baking soda and you should smell a dramatic improvement. If the smell lingers, try the treatment again. You might also try tying the item inside a large garbage bag into which you've sprinkled salt or baking soda; this will help remove any odors lingering on the fabric. When done with either of these treatments, allow the item to sit outside in the sun, if you can, or any place where it can be aired out for a good long time.

If you have stored "keepsake" magazines or newspapers in your garage, with the idea that they might increase in value, think again. None of that is worth anything. Put them out on the curb for recycling or take them to your local recycling center. If you're still not convinced, or perhaps you have a sentimental attachment to your mother's *National Geographic* magazine collection, you can take the musty smell out of each issue by laying them all out in the sun on a dry day (and on a protected surface, obviously). After a good long sunbath, sprinkle them with baking soda, let them sit for an hour or so, and then brush it out. It's a tedious task, but it will do the trick. By the way, the entire collection of *National Geographic* magazine—over 112 years of it—is available in a CD-ROM box set that will take up a lot less space in your garage. Think about it.

...and the rusty

If you have old bicycles or other metal items that have developed a little bit of rust while in storage, you can clean off the rust by mixing up a paste of salt and lemon juice, using 6 parts salt to 2 parts lemon juice. Rub the paste onto the rusted areas with a dry cloth, then rinse and dry thoroughly.

THE GREEN OUTDOORS

Household cleaning tasks will often lead you straight into the out-of-doors, especially if you live in a climate that allows you to use your backyard and patio many months of the year. Green cleaning is a must when cleaning outdoor furniture, grills, and toys. Plus, it's a nice feeling to know you're not harming the environment while you're out there surrounded by it. Once again the Fantastic Four are a huge help, this time with your *outdoor* cleaning. So, let's get started!

Patio furniture

Lawn furniture seems to be a magnet for all the grit and muck that nature can come up with. Outdoor chairs, tables, and loungers can be found caked with dirt, cobwebs, and grease, especially if they've been in storage for a while. Clean them off with a baking soda solution, using 1 cup baking soda added to some warm water. Wipe it on the furniture, then rinse thoroughly.

White wicker furniture is lovely to have for your yard and patio, but it can take a beating if out in the sun too much or left in the rain. You can help keep it from yellowing by scrubbing it periodically with a stiff brush that you have first moistened with salt water. Scrub every nook and cranny in the  chairs and loungers and rinse thoroughly. Then let the pieces sit in the sun to dry, changing their position (upside-down, sideways, etc.) every so often.

THE GREAT OUTDOORS

If you and your family are campers—whether rugged backpackers or vacationers in an environmentally friendly RV—baking soda is a great multipurpose tool to take along with you. You'll be saving valuable space by packing something that can clean just about anything you'll need to clean on your trip (pots, pans, hands, teeth). Start out by using it to deodorize your sleeping bags. Sprinkle them with baking soda and let them sit for a day, then shake out the bags and let them sit in the sun as long as possible. Baking soda is also quite handy for putting out campfires. You can even put an open box of it in an outhouse to deodorize the air. Good luck with that!

On the deck

You know, your garage floor isn't the only place in your home that can be stained by grease and oil—your deck or patio may also be prone to these stains. And as with most cleaning projects, it's best to tackle any stains as soon after the accident as possible.

If your wooden deck has become stained with suntan lotion or grease from an outdoor grill, sprinkle baking soda on it immediately and let it sit an hour. After brushing away the baking soda with a broom, check to see if any of the stain remains. If so, repeat the procedure.

Grills

You'll find all kinds of fancy sprays and specialized formulas in a store for cleaning the burned-on gunk off your outdoor grill racks, but good old elbow grease and a stiff brush are all you really need. It'll help if you can tackle this project when the grill is still a little warm (though not hot!), but it will work regardless.

If you have stubborn charred remains on the racks, try treating those areas with a vinegar and baking soda mix. First apply baking soda and then dab with vinegar to get the foamy action started. Both vinegar and baking soda are safe to use around food, of course, but you'll still want to rinse your grill racks thoroughly before using them again.

Pool toys

If you have a backyard pool or just a collection of beach toys for the kids, you can remove the musty and mildewy smells that may accumulate during the

off-season by washing them with a baking soda solution. Use ¼ cup baking soda for every quart warm water.

Screens

The screens on your home are where the elements—pollution, auto exhaust, tree leaves—stubbornly grab hold. Cleaning them will help you have a brighter outlook onto the outside world from inside your home. Clean your screens by dipping a damp wire brush into baking soda and scrubbing. Then rinse the screens thoroughly with a damp rag or sponge. If you have removed the screens from the windows, use a hose to rinse them.

Siding

If your home has aluminum siding or other aluminum parts, clean them with a baking soda and water solution applied with a soft-bristled brush usually used for car washing. Afterward, rinse clean.

Rust

Say it's spring, and you're taking inventory of your yard and landscape. If you're like many of us (especially many of us with children), perhaps you've found a few things that were left out in the rain and snow when they shouldn't have been. Not to worry—you can clean off any lightly rusted items in an earth-friendly way by using some of the items in our Fantastic Four cleaning kit.

General cleaning

First, mix equal parts salt and cream of tartar, moistened with enough water to make a paste. Use this paste on metal outdoor furniture, for example, or rusted metal parts on an outdoor grill. Apply the paste with a soft cotton cloth and set the item in the sun to dry. Wipe off and repeat if necessary. Afterward, rinse clean. You can also try making this paste using lemon juice and salt, rather than cream of tartar. Be sure

Eco-facts

Approximately nine out of ten newspapers are tossed in the trash instead of recycled.

to keep the amount of lemon juice or water you use consistent with making a paste thick enough to not slide off any vertical surfaces.

Tools 'n' things

If you have a collection of rusty nuts, bolts, and nails sitting around in your workshop, give them a makeover by placing them in a glass jar, filling the jar to about halfway with the metal pieces. Cover the pieces in undiluted vinegar, seal the jar, and let it sit overnight. The next day rinse the pieces thoroughly, and make sure to dry them—after all, we don't want to go through all the work of cleaning just to have them rust up again!

Rusty tools can be revived in a similar way as the nuts and bolts. Place them in a container big enough to hold them as well as enough vinegar to cover them thoroughly, like a plastic bucket or tub. Soak the tools for several hours, then rinse them

---

Eco-facts

Plastic bags are among the most common items of debris found in coastal cleanups.

completely with clean water. Using a cotton cloth, dry them well. If you see the vinegar becoming cloudy before you think the rust has been loosened all the way, change out the vinegar and continue to soak the items.

Puttin' on the Paint

Whether you're tackling a painting project outdoors or inside your home, you can use the Fantastic Four products in a number of ways. When painting in small spaces or enclosed rooms, you can help absorb any paint odors if they bother you or your family by setting out dishes of vinegar. Keep dishes out for a few days after finishing your project, adding new vinegar each day.

Surfaces, particularly metal ones, should always be as clean as possible before applying paint to them. In the past, this has usually meant using a toxic solvent, but vinegar is also a great product to use to truly clean a metal surface. You can achieve the same effect as with a solvent by using 1 part vinegar to 5 parts water. This solution will cut through any dirt or oily residues on the metal, which can really mess with your paint job. It will also make future problems with peeling paint less likely.

Perhaps you didn't clean your brushes properly after using them the last time, and now the bristles have become hardened. Fix this by boiling the brushes in ½ gallon water, 1 cup of baking soda, and ¼ cup vinegar.

Eco-facts

Do the math: Recycling one ton of paper saves 17 Douglas fir trees.

ADDITIONAL RESOURCES

American Association of Poison Control Centers – An organization that promotes safety and knowledge about hazardous materials in the home. Also provides a 24-hour Poison Help hotline. www.aapcc.org/DNN, 1-800-222-1222

Better Basics – A Web site providing homemade recipes (for both food and home care) and solutions for nontoxic, greener living. www.betterbasics.com

Cell Phone Recycling – Check with your provider to see if it has a recycling program. Also try Call2Recycle, www.rbrc.org/call2recycle.

Computer and Electronics Recycling – Check with your manufacturer to see if it has a recycling program. Also try My Green Electronics, www.mygreenelectronics.org.

Earth 911 – Find information on where to recycle various items, as well as tips on living a greener life. http://earth911.org

The Environmental Protection Agency (EPA) – Search its extensive Web site to learn more about the environment and your community, as well as regulations and laws. www.epa.gov

Freecycle – An online community with a focus on swapping and donating new and used products. www.freecycle.org

Green571 – An online community dedicated to sharing information, tips, and support toward living a greener life. Focus is placed on recycling, energy conservation, and the organic lifestyle. Subscribe to the daily e-mail newsletter. www.green571.com

GrassRoots Recycling Network – This nonprofit organization promotes a "Zero Waste" program. The Web site also includes a learning section for kids and teacher materials. www.grrn.org

The Green Guide – A *National Geographic* magazine-related Web site and magazine, featuring green tips, product reviews, and coupons. www.thegreenguide.com

GreenHomeGuide – An online community Web site that provides resources, tips, and articles to help you make your home greener. www.greenhomeguide.com

GreenPeople – An online directory of eco-friendly products, services, and stores. www.greenpeople.org

Green Seal – A nonprofit organization that evaluates and promotes green services and products. www.greenseal.org

Household Products Database – As part of the National Institutes of Health, this Web site provides information and ingredient lists for various cleaning and home maintenance products, including auto, landscaping, pet-care, home-office, and personal-care products.
http://householdproducts.nlm.nih.gov

Mount Sinai Children's Environmental Health Center – Researching the connection between toxic materials in the environment and children's illnesses.
www.childenvironment.org

National Coalition Against Domestic Violence –
Accepting used cell phones as a part of its CALL TO PROTECT
program.
www.ncadv.org/takeaction/donateaphone_129.html

TreeHugger – An online source for green media coverage,
tips, articles, product information, and interviews.
www.treehugger.com

Washington Toxics Coalition – A nonprofit organization
that promotes a healthy public and a healthy environment
through the elimination of toxic pollution. Find articles, tips,
and facts about living a greener, healthier life.
www.watoxics.org